AlphaKids Guided Readers

Teacher Guide for Levels 1–5

alphakids®

Acknowledgements

Susan Hill wishes to thank colleagues at the University of South Australia, and Meridee Cuthill and Val Brittain for their constructive criticism.

Special thanks to Helen Bettes.

Thanks are due to Wendy Bean, Val Delany, Chris Hastwell, Noeleen Stanley, Chris Gray, Eaglehawk Primary School, Mill Park Heights Primary School, Pleasant Street Primary School, and St. Alipius Parish School for reviewing.

Thanks also to Patrick Honan, the Melbourne Zoo, the Jevons family, Heloise and Lillian Meighan, Jessica and Stephanie Pantou, Marcus Richter, Albert Park / South Melbourne Primary School, and Elwood Primary School.

This edition published in North America by
Sundance Publishing
234 Taylor Street
Littleton, MA 01460
800-343-8204

ISBN 0-7608-3460-1

Table of Contents

Meet the AlphaKids

The *AlphaKids* are the 26 children featured in the *AlphaKids Alphabet Books* who make continuing appearances throughout the *AlphaKids Guided Readers*. As a group, the *AlphaKids* represent many cultures and a balance of boys and girls. They are short, tall, silly, serious—like the kids you find in any classroom—and because the *AlphaKids* are real kids, young readers can watch the *AlphaKids* grow up in stories and photos about them, their families, and their friends. Get to know the *AlphaKids* and introduce young readers to a whole alphabet of friends!

Adam

Bob

Cass

Dan

Emma

Fay

Gus

Holly

Izzy

Jake

Kim

Lee

Maria

Nina

Oscar

Patty

Quan

Rose

Sam

Tess

Umberto

Vin

Will

Max

Yoko

Zelda

Guided Readers, Levels 1–5

The AlphaKids Guided Readers, Levels 1–5, offer beginning readers the support and enjoyment they need to take on the exciting challenge of learning to read. Browse through the 30 books in Levels 1–5, and you'll find friendly faces and child-centered topics in a variety of genres that highlight the pleasure and usefulness words and pictures can provide.

How the Program Is Structured

The AlphaKids Guided Readers are designed for guiding young readers, individually or in small groups, through a supported and scaffolded program of literacy development. *Levels 1–5* are for emergent readers. The books in each level offer carefully designed opportunities for beginning readers to acquire knowledge about forms of print and the messages print might carry.

Levels 1–5 of the *AlphaKids Guided Readers* feature:

- 6 emergent reader titles at each level
- a variety of child-centered fiction and nonfiction genres
- gradually increasing challenges in length, language, text format, and story structure
- support for young readers through print placement, repetition of sentence patterns, picture-text correlation, and oral language structures
- leveling that supports Reading Recovery,™ Guided Reading instruction, and teaching plans for at-risk students
- a continuing cast of real and make-believe characters

The Teacher Guide for Levels 1–5 provides:

- information on literacy and emergent reading behaviors
- background information and activities to help children develop in using the four roles of a reader
- 30 step-by-step lesson plans with Guided Reading book introductions, text features for book selection, ongoing tips for observational assessment, and opportunities for tailoring each lesson to children's specific needs as readers
- whole-year learning center plans and book-by-book activities that free teachers to work with small groups
- record forms for taking records of reading behaviors at each level

Level 1

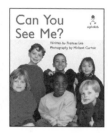
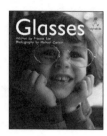

Level 2

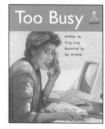

Level 3

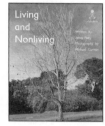

Level 4

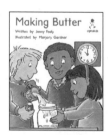

Level 5

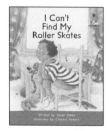

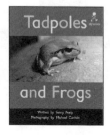

How the Levels Work

AlphaKids Guided Readers provide instructional support through carefully leveled texts that provide a gradual increase in complexity. At the earliest levels, children are given opportunities to attend to word matching, directionality, and high-frequency words. In later levels, young readers must attend more closely to print and notice the distinct features of words and letters. The steady reading progression of *AlphaKids Guided Readers* offers emergent readers measured new challenges and opportunities to grow.

To enjoy the feeling of accomplishment that most motivates young readers, children need a selection of great books at their instructional level. *AlphaKids Guided Readers* were leveled in accordance with the research of Clay, Fountas and Pinnell, and other respected reading practitioners and researchers. The *Guided Readers* support at-risk students, Reading Recovery™, and classroom guided reading groups. Every book was extensively trialed in classrooms and revised until teachers, teacher trainers, and real kids said the books were the best they could be. The list below gives the criteria used to level our books, which teachers also can use to select other books and to focus instruction.

AlphaKids Guided Readers are leveled based on a careful list of criteria:

- complexity of the content
- structure of language and vocabulary
- structure of text and genre
- picture-text correlation
- size and placement of print on a page

Use these detailed features for each level to determine the level at which to place children when starting them out in guided reading. Use the text features found in the lesson plans for each book to select the specific texts you will use.

I like to swing. I like to crawl.

Level 1

- Content very familiar to children
- High-frequency words
- Simple sentence structure
- Predictable, repetitive story line
- Direct match between illustration and text strongly supports the reader
- Consistent layout with ample word spacing
- 8 pages, 1 line of text per page (no return sweep)

Level 2

- ◆ Content familiar to children
- ◆ Additional high-frequency words
- ◆ Sentences begin to vary in length
- ◆ Sentence structure may change slightly on last page
- ◆ Predictable, repetitive story line
- ◆ Illustrations strongly support text
- ◆ Continued ample word spacing
- ◆ 12 pages, 1–3 lines of text per page (introduces return sweep)

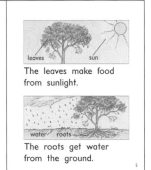

My baby sister can read.
She can read with me.

Level 3

- ◆ Content children can easily relate to
- ◆ Increased list of high-frequency words
- ◆ Increased variation in sentence structure, includes direct speech
- ◆ Opportunities to attend to initial sounds and word endings
- ◆ Illustrations support the text
- ◆ Some variation in picture and text format
- ◆ 12 pages, 1–4 lines of text per page

Can we go fly a kite?

Not now. I'm too busy.

Level 4

- ◆ Concepts children can easily understand
- ◆ Growing list of high-frequency words
- ◆ More variation in sentence structure and language patterns
- ◆ Direct speech, using "said"
- ◆ Illustrations support the text
- ◆ Print on left and right pages, still separate from illustrations
- ◆ 16 pages, 1–7 lines of text per page

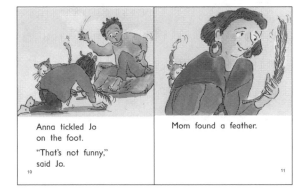

Anna tickled Jo on the foot.
"That's not funny," said Jo.

Mom found a feather.

Level 5

- ◆ Experiences and information children can relate to or imagine
- ◆ Wider range of high-frequency words
- ◆ Increasing variety in sentence length and sentence structure
- ◆ Direct speech using "asked" and "said"
- ◆ Illustrations or labeled diagrams may support or extend text
- ◆ 16 pages, 1–9 lines of text per page

A tree is a plant.
It needs food and water.

leaves   sun
The leaves make food from sunlight.

water   roots
The roots get water from the ground.

The Thinking Behind AlphaKids

The AlphaKids Guided Readers offer young readers authentic opportunities to construct meaning and to problem solve using their newly acquired literacy skills. Each word, each illustration, and the placement of books within each level has been carefully considered and chosen to help young learners. Variety in presentation, topics, and genre enables primary teachers to use *AlphaKids* to support these premises of good first literacy learning.

Literacy Is Integrated

Reading, writing, listening, and speaking all work together in early literacy development. When children *write*, their attention is drawn to how spoken language can be represented in written form. When children *read*, they match their spoken language one-to-one with written text. When children begin to *read and write*, they explore the similarities and differences between spoken and written language. Noticing these similarities and differences helps both forms of language grow; and, in turn, reading acts as a model to extend children's spoken and written language skills.

As children's reading and writing skills grow, so does their fluency with oral and written language. When teachers help children make analogies and integrate information from several sources, children develop those problem-solving strategies and use them in future situations. *AlphaKids* is packed with opportunities for children to notice and investigate the similarities and differences between oral and written language as readers and writers, and as listeners and speakers.

Literacy Development Is Cyclical

Literacy development is a multidimensional process. Literacy development cycles outward, building skills across many dimensions at once. A child who is a fluent reader of caption books can lose fluency when he or she has to puzzle out a new sentence structure. Another child might lose handwriting accuracy as he or she struggles to compose an original sentence. But as children integrate new skills, they regain fluency and form a foundation to support further skills acquisition. A new cycle of development can begin.

AlphaKids enables children to develop skills and strategies in a defined and careful fashion, allowing the child's own strengths to support ongoing success. The teacher's role becomes one of guiding children to experiences that will help them build an integrated foundation of skills.

Literacy Support Should Be Scaffolded

Authentic reading and writing experiences are complex tasks that draw on a variety of skills at any one moment. Building an integrated network of literacy skills takes careful cycling of activities that reinforce learning along the way. Teachers provide the scaffold of support children need to be fluent and flexible in using their literacy skills. They do this by maintaining the complexity of whole tasks while tailoring the demands of the task so that each child is appropriately challenged yet solidly supported. *AlphaKids* provides a flexible structure of meaningful tasks that allow teachers to fine-tune each lesson to each child's needs.

Literacy Should Be Social and Individual

Literacy development is a process of learning about language and the forms, features, and uses of written language. Children learn about literacy from their teacher and their peers. They experience its importance in the world of information around them. However, each child brings a unique skill set to the process of becoming literate. As a result, the challenges each child faces will also be unique. Thoughtful teachers provide a social environment in which young readers can support each other, while allowing them individual time to develop their skills. *AlphaKids* blends together the social setting that supports children as they take on the process of reading and writing and the variety of opportunities that enable teachers to help every child become independent at gaining and sharing information.

Literacy Learning Should Be Child-Centered

Young readers taking on the challenges of attaining literacy skills need validation for their efforts. That comes when teachers select developmentally appropriate activities that are in tune with what children care about. Teachers engage children by selecting texts and activities that inspire and give them a reason to want to learn. Teachers explain, provide information, challenge, question, and observe children's skills and strategies. They help children make connections between books and the world around them. They seek out teaching opportunities by selecting books that offer young readers a chance to grow successfully. As young readers grow, teachers choose opportunities for children to become more and more in control of their own learning path. *AlphaKids* supports teachers by providing the literacy activities and children's texts that recognize and respect the magic of childhood experiences and abilities.

Emergent Reading Behaviors

Emergent Reading

Emergent reading is a process that begins before children come to school and continues into their first years of school. Emergent readers are acquiring conceptual knowledge about the uses of print, and moving toward the point where they can read and write independently.

Emergent readers use four sources of information to make meaning from text:
- **semantics**—the text meaning
- **syntax**—the sentence structure
- **phonology**—the sounds
- **visual**—the print, illustrations, format and layout

Emergent Reading Behaviors

Children use a range of behaviors when they are reading, and the nature of the text will prompt them to integrate information in different ways. Sometimes the illustrations will be of prime importance; at other times decoding a word will be central.

Emergent readers problem solve as they learn to read. They use questions to look for:
- **meaning cues**—*Does that make sense?*
- **structural cues**—*Does that sentence sound right?*
- **visual cues**—*Does that look right?*
- **phonological cues**—*Does that sound right?*

Learning in small groups while using a text at an appropriate level of interest and difficulty helps children to develop these problem-solving behaviors.

Looking for and listening to children's use of reading strategies and their knowledge of print concepts helps teachers plan for appropriate teaching. The listing on page 13 shows some of the emergent reading behaviors that may be observed.

Concepts About Print

- knows where to start
- understands that print records a message
- moves through the text from front to back
- moves left-to-right across the page with a return sweep
- can point to the title
- can point to the author
- can identify the top and bottom of a page
- understands the concept of first, next, and last
- understands the concept of a word
- can identify first, last, next letter
- understands the concept of capital and lowercase letters
- can identify sounds in spoken language
- can identify first, last, next sound in spoken language
- is aware of punctuation: comma, question mark, exclamation mark, quotation mark, period
- understands the concept of a sentence
- can match story and picture
- notices and interprets detail in pictures
- can match word-by-word, indicated by precise pointing
- matches initial sound and letter
- makes one-to-one sound and letter match in written language
- can identify letters of the alphabet
- can identify some high-frequency words

Strategic Thinking

- predicts what makes sense
- makes links between prior knowledge and texts
- integrates several sources of information
- searches illustrations, print, structure, or memory for meaning
- understands some text forms and genres
- uses "book language"
- pays close attention to print, noticing some features of letters and words
- can map several sounds to letters or letter clusters in writing
- can map letters or letter clusters to sounds in reading
- makes a one-to-one match of spoken and written word
- self-corrects when reading
- can make analogies between known words and unfamiliar words
- notices similarities and differences in words
- locates familiar and new words
- persists in problem solving
- selects appropriate books
- remembers familiar sentence structures
- uses knowledge of syntax as a source of information
- self-monitors by using word-by-word matching
- notices known words in a text, or notices mismatches in meaning or language
- explores the author's message in a text

The Four Roles of a Reader

To understand an author's message, a reader needs to approach a new text in many ways, using a variety of integrated skills. Successful readers gather information from text and pictures to find the author's message. They decipher letters, words, punctuation, sentence structure, and syntax to make meaning of what they read. Effective readers go beyond making meaning. They evaluate author and illustrator choices to decide how well the book has fulfilled its purpose. Freebody and Luke have identified *the four roles of a reader* as: meaning maker, code breaker, text user, and text critic.[1]

Even young children need to understand and to experience using all four roles of a reader if they are going to grow into well-rounded, flexible readers. Though the newest readers may not yet be fluent or able to sustain reading for extended periods, they are quite able to have responses to books, to learn the differences between genres, and to share in discussions of a book's success. These activities hold the true purpose for learning to read and the true satisfaction of being a reader.

The four roles of
a reader are:

meaning maker
code breaker
text critic
text user

Every lesson plan offers opportunities for
children to explore all four roles of a reader.

[1] *The four roles of a reader* are based on the work of P. Freebody and A. Luke, "Literacy programs: Debates and Demand in Cultural Context." *Prospect,* 5 (3), 1990, 7–16.

Meaning Maker

Meaning makers read to understand. They search for meaning in the illustrations, the sentence structure, and the print. Before children start a new book, teachers support the role of meaning maker by initiating conversations that build a background that helps children connect the text to their prior experience. Connecting conversations might include:

- building a list of words related to a book's topic
- listing questions about the book's topic
- making semantic webs, mind maps, diagrams
- reading a related poem or story
- sharing experiences about the topic

Teachers continue the support as children read by posing comprehension questions to explore the reader's literal comprehension, inferential comprehension, and critical thinking. Literal comprehension questions concern information clearly stated in print or shown in the illustrations. Inferential comprehension questions require children to read "between the lines" or find clues in the illustrations. Critical thinking questions ask the reader to explore the truth or accuracy of the text.

An Example

For the book *My Baby Sister,* teachers help children extend the meaning of what they have read by using questions such as these:

Meaning makers gather the book's basic message from print and pictures.

What can the baby sister in this book do?

Literal Comprehension Question

Which things does the baby need help to do?

Inferential Comprehension Question

What things can babies do? How do they do them?

Connecting Conversation

How does Nina feel about her baby sister? What makes you think so?

Critical Thinking Question

Code breakers compare words in print to words in speech to confirm meaning.

Code Breaker

Code breakers use what they know about sound-letter relationships, high-frequency sight words, and oral and written language to "decode" what they read. Teachers support the role of code breaker by providing opportunities for children to understand the alphabetic principle, develop phonemic awareness, gain phonics skills, and investigate conventions of print and written language. The alphabetic principle is the connection between the 26 letters of the alphabet and the 44 phonemes, or sounds, that the letters represent. Phonemic awareness, a key factor in understanding the alphabetic principle, is the conscious recognition of individual sounds and words in spoken language. Phonics is the process of analyzing words to determine what sounds each combination of letters represents. Print and written language conventions are the predictable patterns in how books work, how spoken words are represented in type, how punctuation affects meaning, and the grammar, usage, and mechanics of language in print.

Activities to Support Code Breaker Skills

◆ Phonemic awareness activities that promote listening for and responding to sounds, words, syllables, rhyme, alliteration, and specific phonemes.

◆ Letter recognition games that promote learning the letter names, matching upper- and lowercase versions of the same letter, and making connections between a letter and the sound(s) it represents.

◆ Sight-word activities that provide a resource of high-frequency words that children recognize on sight.

◆ Phonics activities that explore word families, onset (the initial sound) and rime (the vowel sound and the consonant sounds that follow it), and ways to use similarities between words to "decode" a new word.

◆ Print and written language activities that explore book handling, word spacing, punctuation, type format and type faces, and oral and literary language conventions as ways to determine whether a decoded word makes sense and sounds right in context.

Text User

Text users identify the form or genre of a book to determine how they will read it. If the book is factual, they focus on reading for information. If a text is fiction, they read to understand the plot, characters, and message of the story. Teachers support the role of text user by providing opportunities for children to investigate how a book is organized, what kind of information a book will share, how presentation affects how a book can be read, possible uses for books of that genre, and how to use that experience to select books for specific purposes.

Text users explore how genre affects the information, the format, and the purpose of a book.

Activities to Support Text User Skills

◆ Ongoing explorations of all forms of print—including worksheets, posters, school announcements, postcards, letters, greeting cards, and environmental print—from which children can analyze the writer's purpose and how the purpose affects the form a message takes.

◆ Activities and games that challenge children to predict the information and format of a book from its title and cover information.

◆ Discussions about why an author wrote a book, how readers might use the book, what kind of readers might like the book, and what other topics might work in that form or genre.

◆ Book-browsing activities that send children to find a book that suits a specific purpose, such as to tell a story, to learn something new, or to find out how to make something.

◆ Book talks and bookmapping activities that help children discover common writing techniques and genre structures, including cumulative tales, circular stories, chronological order, flashbacks, speech and thought bubbles, rhyme, and alliteration.

How will I read this?

◆ Activities, including shared writing, that encourage children to change writing style to suit their purpose for writing.

Text Critic

Text critics evaluate the author's purpose and the author's decisions about how the information is presented. They check for social and cultural fairness, and look for misinformation that misleads the reader. Text critics think about their own response to the book and whether the book is the best it might be. Teachers support the role of text critic by providing opportunities for children to respond to what they read, to add their opinions to the information the author has offered, to challenge the premises put forth as true, and to publish book reviews on their evaluation.

Text critics evaluate what they read, by reading like a writer.

Activities to Support Text Critic Skills

- Ongoing evaluations of print forms that encourage children to decide whether the author has given a clear, fair, and well-organized message that meets the purpose of the work.

- Activities and games that invite children to discuss, share, and recommend books they think are entertaining, informative, and useful.

- Discussions about why an author wrote a book, whether the book meets that purpose, and how the book might be improved.

- Activities that encourage children to evaluate and respond to books and to compare their own opinions with those of other readers.

- Activities that encourage children to critique their own writing and how well they have met their purpose for writing.

Are all children like this?

What does the author think of me?

Assessing Emergent Readers

The primary purpose for assessment is to match each child's instructional experiences to his or her optimum learning level. Starting children in the right place and carefully monitoring their progress is critical to their success as readers. Assessment provides teachers with the information they need to plan and reinforce a child's progress in becoming a skillful reader. Teachers assess each child's prior book experience and early reading accuracy to determine the starting point for that child. They continue to assess each child's progress through formal records of reading behaviors, informal observation, and interaction with children as they work.

Assessing Experience with Books

Teachers can use informal activities to assess each child's experience with books. Some activities to assess a child's experience might include:

- Activities that demonstrate understanding of early print concepts, such as asking children to identify these parts of a book: the top, the bottom, the front, the back, the title, the cover, the writing, a letter, a word, a picture, a page, where to start reading, the direction the words go.

- Activities that demonstrate letter-recognition skills and understanding of the alphabetic principle, such as activities in which children: write or copy their name; say, write, or sing the alphabet; identify some or all letters; name sounds that go with some or all letters; read a list of high-frequency words.

- A home-school questionnaire to determine children's prior experience with books.

Finding the Right Learning Level

Even children with limited book experience can read simple texts, if the teacher is careful to select books at the child's learning level. A learning text is one in which the child feels some challenge, can self-correct, and still demonstrates good comprehension. A child reads with 90–94% accuracy when a book is at his or her learning level. Research has shown that books in which children can achieve 90–94% accuracy provide the approximate challenge that a reader can manage without assistance. Teachers use this information when selecting books for shared reading, guided reading, or independent reading.

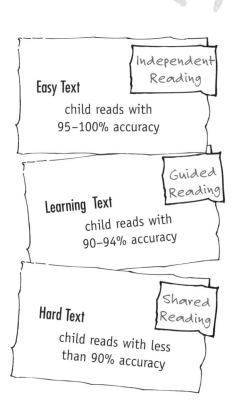

Easy Text
Independent Reading
child reads with 95–100% accuracy

Learning Text
Guided Reading
child reads with 90–94% accuracy

Hard Text
Shared Reading
child reads with less than 90% accuracy

Using Records of Reading Behaviors

To assess ongoing progress, many teachers use a record of reading behaviors. A record of reading behaviors documents a child's performance during the first reading of a new text, including exact errors, miscues, and self-correcting actions. (See pp. 100–101 for how to take a record of reading behaviors.) Teachers analyze the recorded errors, miscues, and self-corrections to determine the reading strategies and behaviors used by that child at a particular point in time.

Records of reading behaviors are taken at regular intervals to help teachers plan for continued instruction and support. Some teachers keep a set of "benchmark books" to use for this process, choosing a book at each level they wish to assess. (See pp. 102–106 for forms to use selected *AlphaKids Guided Readers* to take records of reading behaviors.) However, any book at the child's level that the child has not yet read can provide a chance for a teacher to assess progress through a record of reading behavior. (See p. 107 for a blank form to use with any benchmark book.)

Informal Observation and Interaction

Teachers also use informal techniques to continually assess a child's reading behaviors. The variety of informal assessment techniques include:

- observing a child's silent reading behaviors
- prompting discussions with a child about his or her strategies
- informally listening as a child reads alone or with a group
- monitoring a child's strategies as he or she participates in shared reading
- collecting samples of a child's work for a personal reading portfolio

CHECK THIS

Observe for evidence that children understand print contains messages. Using *Ice Cream*, explain that pictures help us understand print messages. Encourage children to talk about the pictures.

Every Guided Readers Lesson Plan includes a suggestion for informal assessment.

Using the Guided Readers

Using *AlphaKids Guided Readers,* teachers can set up and maintain a balanced, child-centered guided reading program that supports and challenges every young reader. The *AlphaKids* flexible lesson plans help teachers focus their approach on the learner's needs, as they guide children in gaining expertise in all four roles of the reader. The *AlphaKids* literacy center activities engage children so completely that teachers are free to spend "quality" time with individual students and guided reading groups.

What Is Guided Reading?

Within a balanced literacy program, children participate in activities that allow them to imitate, model, practice, share, build skills, make discoveries, and face challenges to extend their literacy.

At the core of these activities is guided reading—the 15 to 30 minute small-group gathering in which children work as apprentice readers under the guidance of their teacher. The small guided reading group is flexible and dynamic, based on a skill set that children share. The building blocks are texts that offer gradually increasing opportunities for learning. The teacher uses insight and observation to match the text to children's needs, and to support children through observing, questioning, modeling, coaching, focusing, and instructing children in the development of flexible reading strategies and problem-solving skills.

Guided Reading teachers support children by observing, questioning, modeling, coaching, and instructing.

Children get opportunities to:
imitate
model
practice
share
build skills
make discoveries
face challenges

A Model for Guided Reading

Teachers are constantly observing individual readers in order to arrange guided reading groups that provide children with the social support of classmates who are ready for similar challenges. Based on the group's skills and strategies, teachers frame the guided reading lesson to meet their needs. Here is a model for preparing and sharing a guided reading lesson.

1. Selecting the Text

Select a text that is related to children's interests and reading behaviors. Read and carefully review the text before the session. Make note of any text features, such as vocabulary, story structure, or syntax, that might be unfamiliar or a challenge to your readers. Choose a focus for the lesson that corresponds to children's reading skills and the text features of the selected book (which can be found in the book's lesson plan).

2. Getting Ready for Reading

Gather the group. Provide a warm-up for reading by helping children connect the book to their own experiences, or plan a simple activity related to the book's ideas that the group can share before reading. Appropriate activities might include discussing, describing, role-playing, playing a simple sharing game, making a chart, brainstorming ideas, or making predictions about the book.

3. Introducing the Book

Book introductions offer an opportunity to custom-fit a book to the needs of a particular guided reading group. Use the book introduction to practice with the group any unfamiliar vocabulary, sentence structure, or syntax in a meaningful context and to focus children's attention on the book's special features. Take care not to read the book for them. Each book requires a slightly different introduction for each group of readers. Depending on the group, teachers might summarize the story line; talk through the illustrations to describe the story line; or page through the book, asking questions about specific pages.

4. Reading the Book

In guided reading, books are selected so that children can read on their own. While children read, you might move from child to child, listening to small sections of text read aloud. Use this opportunity to assess their progress and observe their reading behaviors for ways to further focus your guidance. To encourage children to problem solve words they don't recognize, you might use prompts such as these:

- *What do you expect it will say?*

- *Does that word make sense here?*

- *What word sounds right here?*

- *What clues can you find in the picture?*

- *What other word do you know that starts like this one?*

If a child has particular difficulty, you might set aside time to take a record of reading behaviors and use that to refocus your work together.

KIDS AS...

Meaning Makers   Text Users

Text Critics

Code Breakers

5. Selecting a Focus for Teaching

After children have read the book independently, choose a teaching focus that will help them extend their learning and explore the book's meaning. Select only one or two points of focus for each guided reading session. Use group time to help children explore one or more of the four roles of a reader. This exploration might take different forms with groups at different skill and strategy levels.

For children who need strategies for basic comprehension, you might focus on the roles of meaning maker and code breaker, offering them opportunities to demonstrate comprehension, look for deeper meaning, discuss new vocabulary, find examples of punctuation, or make analogies between new words and words they know. Later, when they have gained fluency and comprehension, you can scaffold their learning by revisiting the text together to explore the roles of text user and text critic.

For children with some comprehension skills and reading fluency, you might explore a different role with each text they encounter, using the opportunities within the text to determine which role of the reader will be the focus that day.

For children who are quick at comprehension and adept at code breaking, you might focus solely on the roles of text user and text critic in order to extend their analytical skills and challenge their ability to read as writers.

Later, you might return to any book or set of books with any group to explore a different role of a reader. Revisiting books with a new focus helps young readers gain flexibility in all four roles of a reader.

6. Using Literacy Learning Centers

Literacy learning centers allow children to practice and consolidate the reading strategies they have learned during guided reading. Set up and introduce several focused centers in the classroom. Provide in the centers independent, open-ended activities that challenge children to take on responsibility for their own literacy. After guided reading, send children to the centers with activities that relate to the book they have just read.

Well-chosen center activities encourage young readers to explore and interact with books in a variety of ways. Introducing activities slowly and changing opportunities over time will keep centers intriguing environments for children to try their skills. To keep centers meaningful to children, remember to provide ample venues for children to share and demonstrate what they have learned, discovered, decided, or made during center time.

Children enjoy a chance to share what they've learned during center time.

How the Lesson Plans Work

Use the *AlphaKids Guided Readers* Lesson Plans to assist in planning and conducting your guided reading lessons. Here's how the lesson plans work.

Getting Ready for Reading
a warm-up activity to help readers make connections to the book

Introducing the Book
tips on preparing readers for the special features of this book

Can You See Me?

Children might recognize the characters in this book from the AlphaKids Alphabet Books.

Caption
alerts teachers to books that include characters children might remember

Text Features
High-Frequency Words
to match the book to the reader's skills

Reading the Book
Selecting a Focus
how to provide guided reading support, and ways to custom fit the lesson to readers' needs

Getting Ready for Reading
Discuss physical features that people have, such as *eyes, ears, nose, teeth, tongue, hair,* and characteristics each feature might have, such as *wavy, curly,* or *straight* hair. Make a chart showing each feature, together with its possible characteristics.

Introducing the Book
You might say:
> This book is a guessing game. Someone on the cover of the book shows you parts of his or her face. You have to decide who it is. First, you see the child's hair, and the child asks, "Can you see my hair?" Then, you see the child's eyes, nose, ear, teeth, and tongue. Can you find the right child?

Reading the Book
As children read independently, listen to each child read small sections of the text and observe reading behaviors for ways to focus your guidance.

Selecting a Focus
Choose the role of the reader, from the *Kids As* menu, that meets the needs of this reading group. Later, you might return to this book to explore another reader's role.

Check This
a quick assessment for readers at this level

Text Features
- This book is a simple guessing game focusing on parts of the head and face.
- Simple, repetitive text
- One line of text per page with no return sweep
- Introduces sentence form *Can you see my _____?*
- Text supported by color photos
- Text placed consistently on page

High-Frequency Words
can, you, see, my, me

CHECK THIS
Observe for evidence that children understand they read from left to right on the page, and they read the left page before the right page. You might say: *Point to where you will start to read. Which page will you read first? Which way will you go?*

LITERACY CENTERS

Writing/Communication Center
Have children make colorful designs that include hidden pictures of their favorite toys. Suggest that they write captions for each picture by completing the sentence form *Can you see my _____?* Allow pairs of children to find their partner's hidden picture.

ABC/Word Center
Provide word cards containing the beginning and ending consonants of the *-an* words. A word card might include *p_n,* and children might write the missing *a* to complete the word. Suggest that they read the words they have created to a friend.

Writing/Communication Center
ABC/Word Center
independent activities that explore the roles of meaning maker and code breaker

44 AlphaKids Guided Readers

KIDS AS Menu
activities for exploring the
Four Roles of a Reader

Meaning Makers
questions that promote reading
comprehension

KIDS AS...

Meaning Makers Use questions like these to explore
with children their role as meaning makers, who gather
the book's basic message from print and pictures.

- *Which child do you think this book is about?*
- *How could you check to be sure you are right?*
- *Which page gave the best clue for finding the right child?*

Code Breakers
activities for vocabulary, word
analysis, and written language skills

Code Breakers Discuss the elements found in this book
to explore with children their role as code breakers, who
investigate print to confirm meaning.

Vocabulary
Word families:
can—ban, Dan, fan, man,
pan, ran, tan, van
my—by, cry, dry, fly, try

Sounds and Letters
Hearing sounds:
/t/—teeth, tongue
long /e/—see, me

Writing Conventions
Punctuation:
question marks, capital
letters to begin sentences
Grammar:
singular and plural—
tooth/teeth, ear/ears
pronouns—me, my

Text Users
questions that help children
learn how books work

Text Users Use questions like these to help children
explore how genre affects the information, the format,
and the purpose of a book.

- *What kind of book is this—fiction or nonfiction?*
  How do you know?
- *Would this book make sense without pictures?*

Text Critics Use questions like these to explore how well the
author and photographer's work has met the book's purpose.

- *What did you like about this book?*
- *If you were the author of the story, what parts of the
  head and face might you include? Why?*

LITERACY CENTERS

Interactive Literacy Center
Have children create clay sculptures of a person.
Direct them to leave out one part of the body, such
as a nose. Have them write the question *Can you see
my _____?* next to their sculpture. Suggest that
children ask a friend to guess what part is missing
and to fill it in on the line. If time allows, provide a
recording of "Head, Shoulders, Knees, and Toes."
Have children act out the movements.

Book Browsing Center
Have children choose a book with photographs
or illustrations of children. Invite them to
select one child from the book to draw. Suggest
that children label the child's features on the
drawings. You might display simple diagrams
with labeled features as a reference.

Text Critics
questions that help children
evaluate an author's work

AlphaKids Guided Readers   **45**

**Interactive Literacy Center
Book Browsing Center**
independent activities that explore all
four roles of a reader and the ways
that readers can respond to books

Managing Guided Reading

The first management problem that faces a guided reading teacher is how to keep the rest of the class learning while she spends quality time working with small groups. Good teachers realize that seatwork activities, such as coloring pictures or filling out worksheets, do little to increase children's literacy skills and can be counterproductive to motivating young readers. To free themselves to work with small groups, many guided reading teachers create centers where children work independently on activities that promote and extend their literacy skills. Literacy centers give teachers the opportunity to focus their attention on small groups and to ensure that, over time, all children investigate a balance of literacy activities and begin to take ownership of their growing literacy skills.

Starting Out

With each new group of children, teachers set up a regular schedule of daily activities and introduce center rules and activities slowly, giving children plenty of time to practice, and plenty of praise for managing their time correctly. As the children learn to work through individual, partner, and small-group activities productively, teachers expand the number and variety of options that children can enjoy during independent literacy time.

To get started, you might try working with only one or two guided reading groups a day. Begin with a whole-group activity, such as a Read-Aloud or Shared Reading. Follow that with an introduction to a literacy task children can do on their own, such as silently reading a self-selected book. Ask children to complete the task independently, while you work with one guided reading group. Offer a suggestion, such as writing a journal response or choosing another book to read, for children to move on to should they finish their assigned work early. When you finish with the first guided reading group, return to the class to comment on their success. Then offer children another repeating task (or another chance at the first task), while you work with a second group. If the routine stays constant, children will quickly learn how independent literacy time should work.

With a Little Experience

By offering children more responsibility for their independent work, in a short time, you will be able to work with three or four groups a day. Again, setting up a routine makes management easier for both the teacher and the class. You might continue to start with whole-group literacy activities. Now, you might offer children two or three tasks that they are expected to accomplish that day, while you work with guided reading groups. Some teachers use an Activity Board (see p. 31) to help children manage their list of tasks. A sample list might include: read a book and make a drawing or journal entry about the book, listen to a book in the listening center, make a list of words that have three letters. One day each week, you might use this whole-group time to introduce a new literacy center (see pp. 30–31) or to present the new activities a center offers. Allow small groups to practice using the new center as one of that day's assigned tasks. Before you know it, children will be able to participate in a variety of assigned and optional tasks that extend and promote their growing literacy.

Whole-Group Activities

- Read-aloud story
- Shared Reading
- Shared Writing
- Reading the room together
- Sharing a new center activity
- Vocabulary, phonics, word, or alphabet games
- "How-to" sessions on selecting books, using the audiotapes, or journal writing.

Whole-group activities introduce children to what will later be an independent activity.

Independent Tasks

- Read a self-chosen book
- Share a book with a friend
- Draw a picture about a book
- Write a journal entry about a book
- Find and list words that begin a specific letter
- Use letter cards to make a word list
- Read around the room
- Draw pictures of words that rhyme
- Make a bookmark, book cover, or a storybook

Independent activities keep kids engaged, and free the teacher to work with small groups.

Using Literacy Learning Centers

Literacy learning centers are classroom areas set up to allow children to practice and extend the learning introduced in a guided reading session. In a literacy center, children engage in purposeful, authentic literacy activities, such as partner reading, word games, simple reader's theater, making books. The activities in a literacy center offer opportunities for children to work cooperatively in small groups, as partners, and as individuals sharing a center's materials.

Making Centers a Success

To ensure children are successful and productive in centers, teachers carefully select and introduce center activities that children can work on without assistance from the teacher. Often teachers will practice a game or activity with a group before making it part of a center's list of activities. This gives the teacher a chance to ensure that children understand the rules of the game well enough to work together without conflict or confusion. Many teachers begin slowly, introducing children to the activities in one center over a period of days before moving on to the next center.

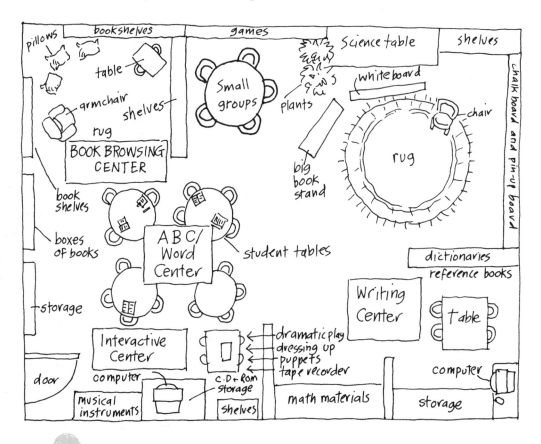

AlphaKids Guided Readers

Guided Reading Groups and Activity Groups

Groups for guided reading are highly flexible and need to remain dynamic. Guided reading groups bring together children with similar strengths who are ready for similar challenges. Children move out of a group as they gain the skills that group is working on, and into a new group to share new challenges. Groups for center activities should be dynamic and flexible as well, but the focus becomes providing children with social and intellectual diversity that offers support and challenge for every child.

When first getting to know a new group of children, you might form guided reading groups of children with similar skills and have these groups stay together, following the same schedule for center activities. This allows children to learn a less complicated routine and allows you to bring a whole group to the guided reading session. Very soon, however, you will find it more beneficial to have children share collaborative activities with a more diversified group, and to call children from several groups to a guided reading session.

Using Activity Boards

To help children manage their time productively, set up an Activity Board that shows how each group will rotate through a balance of activities each day. Introduce the Activity Board sign for each literacy center as you introduce that center. Doing so will help children become familiar with how the Activity Board works. Each morning you might also review with each group what centers will be part of their day. As always, starting slowly helps. If a teacher is working with four literacy center groups and four centers, a weekly Activity Board might look like this:

Adam, Bob, Cass, Dan, Emma	Fay, Gus, Holly, Izzy, Jake
ABC/Word Center	Book Browsing Center
Writing/Communication Center	ABC/Word Center
Interactive Literacy Center	Writing/Communication Center
Book Browsing Center	Interactive Literacy Center
Kim, Lee, Maria, Nina, Oscar	**Patty, Quan, Rose, Sam, Tess**
Interactive Literacy Center	Writing/Communication Center
Book Browsing Center	Interactive Literacy Center
ABC/Word Center	Book Browsing Center
Writing/Communication Center	ABC/Word Center

When children are ready for more choices add optional activities:

- Read around the room.
- Read at the overhead projector.
- Make a recording of today's book.
- Make a book, card, letter, or bookmark.

The Writing/Communication Center

The *Writing/Communication Center* offers children a workplace in which they can explore how oral/written language relationships work and how we use written language and art to communicate meaning. For early readers, work in this center might include innovating on text they have read, responding to a book by writing or drawing, or trying their hand at creating something new.

Encourage children to use the *Writing/Communication Center* to express their ideas and to practice how writing works. Invite them to display their work in the center and share it with the class. As always, introduce the center slowly, allowing children limited options to explore. As the year progresses and children become more familiar with the center, introduce new materials and new options to match their growing skills.

To supply your *Writing/Communication Center,* you might ask parents or local businesses to contribute some of the things you need. Materials you might keep at the *Writing/Communication Center* include:

paper of every size, kind, and color:

- ☐ writing journals for each child
- ☐ lined paper
- ☐ unlined paper
- ☐ blank books
- ☐ construction paper
- ☐ oaktag
- ☐ poster board
- ☐ adding machine paper
- ☐ old wallpaper books
- ☐ note cards
- ☐ stationery
- ☐ envelopes
- ☐ memo forms
- ☐ index cards
- ☐ to-do lists
- ☐ postcards
- ☐ phone message pads

writing and drawing tools of every size, kind, and color:

- ☐ pencils
- ☐ pens
- ☐ markers
- ☐ crayons
- ☐ paints and brushes
- ☐ safety scissors
- ☐ glue
- ☐ tape
- ☐ safety stapler
- ☐ print/picture stamp pad set
- ☐ magazines and catalogs to cut up for pictures and words
- ☐ old typewriter
- ☐ computer and printer
- ☐ chalk and chalkboard

reference materials:

- ☐ dictionaries
- ☐ word lists
- ☐ encyclopedias
- ☐ alphabet posters
- ☐ spelling lists
- ☐ proofreading list
- ☐ samples of a variety of writing genres

real writing samples:

- ☐ children's magazines
- ☐ newspapers
- ☐ catalogs
- ☐ pamphlets
- ☐ lists
- ☐ greeting cards
- ☐ letters
- ☐ postmarked envelopes
- ☐ postcards
- ☐ recipe cards
- ☐ memos
- ☐ menus
- ☐ comic strips
- ☐ phone messages
- ☐ coupons
- ☐ bookmarks
- ☐ award certificates

Things to Do in the Writing / Communication Center

♦ **Write a book or story about something real.**

yourself	*a game or party*
your friends	*a trip*
your family	*buildings*
a book	*plants*
animals	*weather*
food	*shoes*

♦ **Write in your journal.**

♦ **Write a book report.**

♦ **Write a letter to a friend.**

♦ **Write a letter to your favorite author.**

♦ **Write a recipe.**

♦ **Write a weather report.**

♦ **Write how to do something.**

♦ **Write a secret message.**

♦ **Write a poem.**

♦ **Write a song.**

♦ **Write a riddle.**

♦ **Write a list of things to do.**

♦ **Write a silly phone message for a friend.**

♦ **Make a thank-you note.**

♦ **Make a postcard.**

♦ **Write a book or story about something make-believe.**

an alien spaceship
a monster in a cave
a robot teacher
a pet dragon
talking animals
talking plants
a trip to the moon
a strange adventure
a backward day
a house on wheels
weird weather
a silly school

♦ **Make a greeting card.**

♦ **Make an award certificate.**

♦ **Make a menu.**

♦ **Make a bookmark for a book.**

♦ **Make a comic strip.**

♦ **Make a new cover for a book you like.**

♦ **Make an ad for a newspaper.**

♦ **Make a poster about something you like.**

♦ **Draw a picture and write a story about it.**

♦ **Draw a character you would like to read about.**

The ABC/Word Center

The *ABC/Word Center* offers children a workplace in which to explore language at the word level—sound/letter relationships, how letters form words, and how words form sentences. For early readers, work in the *ABC/Word Center* might include visual discrimination games, letter/sound work, word and sentence construction, or finding examples of what they have learned. Many teachers also keep an ongoing word wall on butcher paper to record words children are learning.

Encourage children to use the *ABC/Word Center* to explore the decoding of written language and to find patterns to guide them as they read and write. Invite children to work together in the center to share in games and activities that help them practice the mechanics of language. As always, introduce the center slowly, allowing children limited options to explore. As the year progresses and children become more familiar with the center, introduce new materials and new options to match their growing skills.

To supply the *ABC/Word Center,* you might ask parents or local businesses to contribute some of the things you need. Materials you might keep at the *ABC/Word Center* include:

letters, words, labels, and counters to mark word parts of every size and kind:

- ☐ letter cards
- ☐ magnetic letters
- ☐ felt letters and flannel board
- ☐ bulletin board letters
- ☐ flashcards
- ☐ colorful counters
- ☐ letter and word games
- ☐ matching and memory games
- ☐ labels naming each area of the center and classroom
- ☐ tapes of alphabet songs and recorder
- ☐ sound boxes for sorting objects by sound

writing and drawing tools of every size, kind, and color:

- ☐ pencils
- ☐ pens
- ☐ markers
- ☐ crayons
- ☐ safety scissors
- ☐ glue
- ☐ tape
- ☐ safety stapler
- ☐ print/picture stamp pad set
- ☐ magazines and catalogs to cut apart for pictures and words
- ☐ chalk and chalkboard
- ☐ white board and markers
- ☐ old typewriter
- ☐ computer and printer

paper of every size, kind, and color:

- ☐ removable labels
- ☐ letter cards
- ☐ word cards
- ☐ sentence strips
- ☐ "sticky notes"
- ☐ lined paper
- ☐ unlined paper
- ☐ blank books
- ☐ construction paper
- ☐ oaktag
- ☐ adding machine paper

reference materials:

- ☐ alphabet books
- ☐ alphabet posters
- ☐ pictionaries
- ☐ dictionaries
- ☐ word lists
- ☐ alphabet songs on tape and a tape recorder with headsets

Things to Do in the ABC/Word Center

◆ **Do these to make a special set of alphabet cards.**

Draw a robot or an animal that looks like one letter of the alphabet on each card.

Make a set of alphabet cards with the consonants in one color and the vowels in another.

Make one set of alphabet cards in small letters and one set in capital letters.

◆ **Do these things with alphabet cards.**

Make words you can read.

Make words you just learned.

Make words that start with the same letter.

Make words that rhyme.

Make up a game using alphabet cards. Teach it to a friend.

◆ **Write the alphabet in your best handwriting.**

◆ **Read an alphabet book.**

◆ **Find all of the letters of your name in a book.**

◆ **Count how many letters of your name are in someone else's name, too.**

◆ **Make a special set of word cards. Ask a friend to guess how you picked the words.**

◆ **Cut out words and letters from old magazines to write a sentence.**

◆ **Do one of these to make an ABC book.**

On each letter page, paste 25 examples of that letter you have cut from old magazines.

On each letter page, write a rhyme or riddle about something that starts with that letter.

On each letter page, write all of the words you can think of that start with that letter.

◆ **Write every three-letter word you can think of.**

◆ **Do these things with a friend and two books you both can read. Take turns.**

See whose book has the most letters.

See whose book has the most words.

See whose book has the longest word.

See whose book has the most sentences.

See whose book has the longest sentence.

Pick a letter. See whose book has the most words with that letter.

Read a sentence. Have your friend put down a counter for each word.

Read a sentence. Have your friend put down a counter for each syllable.

Read a sentence. Have your friend find the sentence in your book.

◆ **Play an ABC or word game in the center.**

◆ **Add words to the word wall that are not there.**

The Interactive Literacy Center

The *Interactive Literacy Center* offers children a workplace in which to explore meaning and expression—how written words sound when read, how stories are structured, and how authors can share meaning in a variety of venues. For early readers, work in the *Interactive Literacy Center* might include listening to audiotapes of books, reading and recording a book on tape, retelling or acting out a story, or creating a skit in which a child interviews characters from a story. Many teachers keep costumes and props in the center to promote dramatic play.

Encourage children to use the *Interactive Literacy Center* to explore speaking, listening, and reading with expression, as well as story-telling. Invite children to use movement, expression, and a range of voices appropriately as they read, perform, and retell stories. As always, introduce the center slowly, allowing children limited options to explore. As the year progresses and children become more familiar with the center, introduce new materials and new options to match their growing skills.

To supply the *Interactive Literacy Center,* you might ask parents or local businesses to contribute some of the things you need. Materials you might keep at the *Interactive Literacy Center* include:

costumes and props or things that can be used as:

- ☐ hats
- ☐ shoes
- ☐ shawls
- ☐ masks
- ☐ outerwear
- ☐ frames for glasses
- ☐ housekeeping props
- ☐ office props
- ☐ restaurant props
- ☐ things to use as microphones and movie/TV cameras

materials for simple scenery, masks, and signs:

- ☐ markers
- ☐ crayons
- ☐ a variety of art supplies
- ☐ butcher paper
- ☐ safety scissors
- ☐ glue
- ☐ tape
- ☐ large and small cardboard boxes
- ☐ overhead projector and supplies
- ☐ flannel board and story pieces for reenacting stories
- ☐ paper dolls and backdrops for reenacting stories

listening and recording materials:

- ☐ tape recorder and headsets
- ☐ instructions for using the recording equipment
- ☐ blank tapes for recording children as they read with expression
- ☐ books and cassettes for listening

reference materials:

- ☐ simple plays
- ☐ fairy tales
- ☐ storybooks
- ☐ picture books
- ☐ videocassette recorder and videos of children's classics

Things to Do in the Interactive Literacy Center

◆ **To enjoy a tape, do one of these.**

Listen to a story tape. Tell a friend your favorite part.

Make a tape recording.

Record yourself reading a book. Listen to how you read.

Record yourself reading something you wrote. Listen to how you read.

Record a story with a friend. Use different voices for the characters.

Record a story while pretending you are a newscaster on TV.

◆ **To read with a partner, do one of these.**

Take turns reading each page.

Ask each other questions about the story.

Take turns acting out what your partner reads.

Tell each other about the parts you like best.

Tell each other about the characters you like best.

Take turns reading like a teacher might read.

Use a factual book. Take turns reading like a scientist might read.

◆ **To share a book with everyone, work with a friend and do one of these.**

Make up a song about a book you both like.

Make a poster about a book you both like.

Make a commercial about a book you both like.

Act out the best part of a book you both like.

◆ **To retell a story, do one of these.**

Use the pictures in a book you like to tell a story.

Draw a story map about a book you like. Use it to retell the story to a friend.

Retell a story to a friend. Give the story a new ending.

Pretend you are a newscaster. Retell a story as if you are on TV.

Pretend you are a talk show host. Have your friend tell you a story.

Pretend you are a story character. Invite a friend to guess who you are.

◆ **To make up new stories, work with a friend and do one of these.**

Act out a story for a friend. Let your friend guess what story it is.

Act out a story you both like. Then act out what might happen next.

Pretend you are making a silent movie. Act out a story without using words.

Act out a make-believe party and be your favorite character.

The Book Browsing Center

The *Book Browsing Center* offers children a workplace in which to explore a variety of books. For early readers, work in the *Book Browsing Center* might include selecting a book to read silently, browsing to find a book for a specific purpose, or discussing a book with a classmate. Naturally, the books set aside for independent reading should offer a wide range of titles that children can read successfully. Many teachers also include a selection of above-level books for children to explore for a specific purpose, such as browsing encyclopedias to find animal pictures, or browsing a selection of nonfiction to compare contents pages. This early exploration helps children to feel comfortable with all kinds of books and to develop intuitive patterns about how books work.

Encourage children to use the *Book Browsing Center* to gain experience in selecting books, to practice their reading skills, and to explore the variety of ways in which books can be used. To supply the *Book Browsing Center,* you might ask parents or local businesses to contribute some of the things you need. Materials you might keep at the *Book Browsing Center* include:

books of every size and kind:

- ☐ books for independent reading
- ☐ big books and read-alouds you have shared with the class
- ☐ storybooks
- ☐ fairy tales
- ☐ folktales
- ☐ concept books
- ☐ cookbooks
- ☐ how-to books
- ☐ photo-essay books
- ☐ humor books
- ☐ poetry
- ☐ plays
- ☐ a range of nonfiction
- ☐ songbooks
- ☐ pictionaries
- ☐ dictionaries
- ☐ encyclopedias
- ☐ almanacs
- ☐ diaries and calendars
- ☐ telephone books
- ☐ class-made books
- ☐ children's magazines and newspapers

color-coded signs/book spine tape and containers to separate book types:

- ☐ for each level of independent reading books
- ☐ for reference books
- ☐ for big books
- ☐ for read-alouds
- ☐ for fiction
- ☐ for nonfiction
- ☐ for class-made books
- ☐ for poetry
- ☐ for plays and songbooks
- ☐ for telephone books
- ☐ for children's magazines and newspapers

furnishings and props to make reading fun:

- ☐ small tables with chairs
- ☐ beanbag chairs
- ☐ comfy pillows
- ☐ air mattress
- ☐ big book easel
- ☐ rocking chair
- ☐ magnifying glasses
- ☐ "reading" hats and soft earmuffs to quiet the sound
- ☐ stuffed animals or book characters as "reading friends"

helpful additions:

- ☐ a map of the center to show where each kind of book belongs
- ☐ display area for books and shared reading work
- ☐ posters that encourage reading
- ☐ an opinion wall or chart for children to rate books they have read

Things to Do in the Book Browsing Center

- **Read a book like these by yourself.**

  a book you've read

  a book you've never read

  a book about something you do

  a book a friend told you about

  a storybook

  a factual book

  a funny book

  a word book

  a book about food

  a book about animals

  a book about a family

  a book about a game

- **Read a book like these with a friend.**

  your favorite book

  your friend's favorite book

  a book you both like

  a book the class made

  an alphabet book

  a counting book

  a rhyming book

  a how-to book

  a book about people

  a book about a place

  a book about a problem

  a book about a party

- **Read something in a magazine. Tell a friend about what you read.**

- **Read something in a newspaper. Tell a friend about what you read.**

- **Choose a book your teacher read aloud. Retell the story to a friend.**

- **Look in an encyclopedia for something you know about.**

- **Look at a pictionary and a dictionary. See how they are the same. See how they are different.**

- **Find a word in a pictionary. Look in a dictionary to find the same word.**

- **Find two books by the same author. Read the books to see how they are the same.**

- **Find two books with the same character. Read the books to see how they are different.**

- **Find a factual book and a fiction book about the same thing. Read them to see which book you like best.**

- **Look through a cookbook with a friend. Find a food you would both like to eat.**

- **Write in your journal about a book you read today.**

- **Write about a book on the class opinion chart.**

- **Write the names of two books you will read tomorrow.**

- **Write a letter to your favorite author.**

Fruit Salad

Getting Ready for Reading

Share your favorite fruit with the children. Ask children, individually, to share their favorite fruit. Use the chant *I like* (*fruit of their choice*).

Introducing the Book

Talk through the book, discussing the fruit that the writer likes. Model the form of the *I like* _____ sentence. You might say:

> This is a book about the fruit the author, Frances Lee, likes to eat. She tells us, "I like apples. I like oranges." On each page, she tells about a fruit that she likes.

Reading the Book

As children read independently, listen to each child read small sections of the text and observe reading behaviors for ways to focus your guidance.

Selecting a Focus

Choose the role of the reader, from the *Kids As* menu, that meets the needs of this reading group. Later, you might return to this book to explore another reader's role.

Text Features

- This book lists some of the fruit that can be used to make fruit salad.
- Simple, repetitive text
- One line of text per page with no return sweep
- Introduces sentence form *I like* _____.
- Text supported by color photos
- Text placed consistently on page

High-Frequency Words

I, like

CHECK THIS

Observe children's book handling skills. Talk about front cover, back cover, title page, and where to start reading. If necessary, point to the front of the book and then to the back of the book. Next, ask: *Where will we start reading?*

LITERACY CENTERS

Writing/Communication Center
Provide pictures of fruits and matching word cards. Have children match the name of the fruit with its picture. Suggest that they draw a bowl around the pictures and word cards to hold the contents.

ABC/Word Center
Have children read the room to find as many words beginning with the initial sound of /p/ as they can. Suggest that children write their words on a chart that you may discuss later.

KIDS AS...

Meaning Makers Use questions like these to explore with children their role as meaning makers, who gather the book's basic message from print and pictures.

- ◆ *Which fruits are in the fruit salad?*
- ◆ *What size bowl might be needed to hold this fruit salad?*

Code Breakers Discuss the elements found in this book to explore with children their role as code breakers, who investigate print to confirm meaning.

Vocabulary
Word families:
Recognize word families:
like—bike, hike

Writing Conventions
Punctuation:
capital letters and periods

Sounds and Letters
Hearing sounds:
/p/—pears, peaches
(other fruits: pineapples,
papayas)

Text Users Use questions like these to help children explore how genre affects the information, the format, and the purpose of a book.

- ◆ *What does this book help you to learn about fruit salad?*
- ◆ *What other kinds of books would have information about making a fruit salad?*

Text Critics Use questions like these to explore how well the author and photographer's work has met the book's purpose.

- ◆ *What other fruits could have been included?*
- ◆ *Which of your friends would like this book? Why do you think so?*

LITERACY CENTERS

Interactive Literacy Center
Have children bring fruits to life as puppets. Provide craft sticks, crayons, construction paper, and glue to make fruit on a stick. Have pairs of children create a conversation that fruits might have with each other. Suggest the dialogue be performed as a puppet show.

Book Browsing Center
Have children locate books about their favorite foods. Invite them to write the titles on a chart entitled *You Might Like to Read About . . .* to recommend books to their friends.

Ice Cream

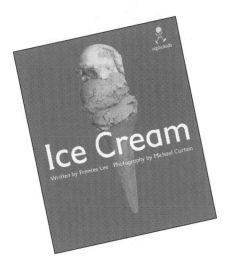

Text Features

- This book uses ice cream to explore color.
- Simple, repetitive text
- One line of text per page with no return sweep
- Introduces sentence form *This is _____ ice cream.*
- Text supported by color photos
- Text placed consistently on page

High-Frequency Words

This, is, my

Getting Ready for Reading

Ask: *Who likes ice cream?* Have children talk about flavors of ice cream they prefer. Encourage children to describe how their favorite ice cream looks and tastes. You might want to list their ideas on an experience chart for Shared Reading.

Introducing the Book

Talk through the book by modeling the form of the text. You might say:

> *We usually talk about ice cream flavors, but this book is about colors of ice cream. This is white ice cream. What other colors can you see?*

Reading the Book

As children read independently, listen to each child read small sections of the text and observe reading behaviors for ways to focus your guidance.

Selecting a Focus

Choose the role of the reader, from the *Kids As* menu, that meets the needs of this reading group. Later, you might return to this book to explore another reader's role.

CHECK THIS

Observe for evidence that children understand print contains messages. Using *Ice Cream*, explain that pictures help us understand these messages. Encourage children to talk about the pictures.

LITERACY CENTERS

Writing/Communication Center
Provide restaurant menus for children to browse. Challenge children to write pages for their own ice-cream menu. Have them complete the sentence form *This is _____ ice cream.* with other colors or flavors of ice cream.

ABC/Word Center
Provide color words—*red, orange, yellow, white, blue*—on paper of the appropriate color. Place the color words on the floor to make a floor chart. Invite children to find pictures in magazines, cut them out, and add them to the chart according to their color.

KIDS AS...

Meaning Makers Use questions like these to explore with children their role as meaning makers, who gather the book's basic message from print and pictures.

- *What colors does this book talk about?*
- *What do you find out about the writer's favorite ice cream?*

Code Breakers Discuss the elements found in this book to explore with children their role as code breakers, who investigate print to confirm meaning.

Vocabulary
Color words:
red, orange, yellow, white,
blue, green

Sounds and Letters
Hearing words:
Children clap when they
hear a specified word or
to indicate the number
of words in a sentence.

    ★ ★ ★ ★ ★
This is white ice cream.

Hearing sounds:
long /i/—ice cream, white
soft /c/—ice
hard /c/—cream

Writing Conventions
Punctuation:
capital letters and periods

Text Users Use questions like these to help children explore how genre affects the information, the format, and the purpose of a book.

- *What does this book help you find out about?*
- *What would you expect to find in a book like this that was called* Shoes?

Text Critics Use questions like these to explore how well the author and photographer's work has met the book's purpose.

- *Do you think someone who did not like ice cream might enjoy this book? Why do you think so?*

LITERACY CENTERS

Interactive Literacy Center
Encourage children to use the ice-cream menus they created at the *Writing/Communication Center* as they act out the roles of customer and waiter/waitress at an ice-cream shop. Invite them to create a jingle for the ice-cream shop and record it on a cassette tape. If possible, provide aprons and paper hats as costumes.

Book Browsing Center
Have children search for books about a variety of objects: foods, kinds of homes, and so on. On a chart entitled *Many Kinds of . . .* , have children write the book title and the number of objects featured in the book they chose.

Can You See Me?

Children might recognize the characters in this book from the AlphaKids Alphabet Books.

Text Features

- This book is a simple guessing game focusing on parts of the head and face.
- Simple, repetitive text
- One line of text per page with no return sweep
- Introduces sentence form *Can you see my _____?*
- Text supported by color photos
- Text placed consistently on page

High-Frequency Words

can, you, see, my, me

Getting Ready for Reading

Discuss physical features that people have, such as *eyes, ears, nose, teeth, tongue, hair,* and characteristics each feature might have, such as *wavy, curly,* or *straight* hair. Make a chart showing each feature, together with its possible characteristics.

Introducing the Book

You might say:

> *This book is a guessing game. Someone on the cover of the book shows you parts of his or her face. You have to decide who it is. First, you see the child's hair, and the child asks, "Can you see my hair?" Then, you see the child's eyes, nose, ear, teeth, and tongue. Can you find the right child?*

Reading the Book

As children read independently, listen to each child read small sections of the text and observe reading behaviors for ways to focus your guidance.

Selecting a Focus

Choose the role of the reader, from the *Kids As* menu, that meets the needs of this reading group. Later, you might return to this book to explore another reader's role.

CHECK THIS

Observe for evidence that children understand they read from left to right on the page, and they read the left page before the right page. You might say: *Point to where you will start to read. Which page will you read first? Which way will you go?*

LITERACY CENTERS

Writing/Communication Center

Have children make colorful designs that include hidden pictures of their favorite toys. Suggest that they write captions for each picture by completing the sentence form *Can you see my _____?* Allow pairs of children to find their partner's hidden picture.

ABC/Word Center

Provide word cards containing the beginning and ending consonants of the *-an* words. A word card might include *p_n,* and children might write the missing *a* to complete the word. Suggest that they read the words they have created to a friend.

KIDS AS...

Meaning Makers Use questions like these to explore with children their role as meaning makers, who gather the book's basic message from print and pictures.

- *Which child do you think this book is about?*
- *How could you check to be sure you are right?*
- *Which page gave the best clue for finding the right child?*

Code Breakers Discuss the elements found in this book to explore with children their role as code breakers, who investigate print to confirm meaning.

Vocabulary
Word families:
can—ban, Dan, fan, man,
pan, ran, tan, van
my—by, cry, dry, fly, try

Sounds and Letters
Hearing sounds:
/t/—teeth, tongue
long /e/—see, me

Writing Conventions
Punctuation:
question marks, capital
letters to begin sentences
Grammar:
singular and plural—
tooth/teeth, ear/ears
pronouns—me, my

Text Users Use questions like these to help children explore how genre affects the information, the format, and the purpose of a book.

- *What kind of book is this—fiction or nonfiction? How do you know?*
- *Would this book make sense without pictures?*

Text Critics Use questions like these to explore how well the author and photographer's work has met the book's purpose.

- *What did you like about this book?*
- *If you were the author of the story, what parts of the head and face might you include? Why?*

LITERACY CENTERS

Interactive Literacy Center
Have children create clay sculptures of a person. Direct them to leave out one part of the body, such as a nose. Have them write the question *Can you see my _____?* next to their sculpture. Suggest that children ask a friend to guess what part is missing and to fill it in on the line. If time allows, provide a recording of "Head, Shoulders, Knees, and Toes." Have children act out the movements.

Book Browsing Center
Have children choose a book with photographs or illustrations of children. Invite them to select one child from the book to draw. Suggest that children label the child's features on the drawings. You might display simple diagrams with labeled features as a reference.

Glasses

Children might remember Emma as the child in the *AlphaKids Alphabet Book for E.*

Text Features

- This book is about a family in which every member wears glasses.
- Simple, repetitive text
- One line of text per page with no return sweep
- Introduces sentence form *My _____ has glasses.*
- Text supported by color photos
- Text placed consistently on page

High-Frequency Words

My, has

Getting Ready for Reading

Show pictures of different kinds of glasses, such as sunglasses and reading glasses. Discuss why people wear glasses.

Introducing the Book

Show the cover of *Glasses.* You might say:

> *This is a book about Emma and her family. Her family is special because they all wear glasses. The book is written as if Emma is talking to us and telling us about her family. She says, "My dad has glasses." You might say, "Her dad has glasses."*

Reading the Book

As children read independently, listen to each child read small sections of the text and observe reading behaviors for ways to focus your guidance.

Selecting a Focus

Choose the role of the reader, from the *Kids As* menu, that meets the needs of this reading group. Later, you might return to this book to explore another reader's role.

CHECK THIS

Observe for evidence that children can match a printed word with a spoken word as they read. To promote this, you might say: *As you read, match the words with what you say.*

LITERACY CENTERS

Writing/Communication Center

Have children imagine and draw a robot family that has one characteristic in common. Challenge children to write a short text about the robot family, using the sentence form *My _____ has _____.* Encourage children to be creative and to share their finished work with a friend.

ABC/Word Center

Write *family, grandpa, my,* and *glasses* on word cards, cut them into syllables, and place the cards into an envelope. Make several sets of syllables into an envelope. Make several sets of cards. Invite pairs of children to put the syllables back together to form the original words. Then, have them count the syllables in each word.

KIDS AS...

Meaning Makers Use questions like these to explore with children their role as meaning makers, who gather the book's basic message from print and pictures.

- *How are the members of Emma's family alike?*
- *How are the members of Emma's family different?*
- *How are many families like this one? How are they different?*

Code Breakers Discuss the elements found in this book to explore with children their role as code breakers, who investigate print to confirm meaning.

Vocabulary
Word awareness:
singular and plural—
glass/glasses
Word families:
Dad—bad, glad, had, mad, sad

Sounds and Letters
Hearing words:
syllables—Children can clap when they hear the beat in these words.

★ ★ ★   ★   ★ ★   ★ ★
fam-i-ly grand-pa my glass-es

Writing Conventions
Punctuation:
capital letters and periods

Text Users Use questions like these to help children explore how genre affects the information, the format, and the purpose of a book.

- *Do you think this book is about a real family or a make-believe family? How can you tell?*

Text Critics Use questions like these to explore how well the author and photographer's work has met the book's purpose.

- *What do you think the author thinks about wearing glasses?*
- *What might the author do to make the book more fun?*

LITERACY CENTERS

Book Browsing Center
Have children select a book about a family and share it with a friend. Suggest that children write their feelings, opinions, or comments about the book of their choice in their personal notebook.

Interactive Literacy Center
Provide frames of discarded glasses for children to try on. Have them take turns reading *Glasses* aloud, while their classmates act out the part of each family member. Include Marc Brown's book *Arthur's Eyes*, on cassette tape for children to listen to, if time allows.

Dogs

Text Features

- This book explores the opposite attributes of dogs.
- Simple, repetitive text
- One line of text per page with no return sweep
- Introduces sentence form *This is a _____ dog.*
- Text supported by color photos
- Text placed consistently on page

High-Frequency Words

This, is, a, big, little, my

Getting Ready for Reading

Talk about dogs children own or know. *What do the dogs look like? What characteristics do they have?* Brainstorm with children pairs of opposite words that could describe dogs, such as *big/little; fat/thin; happy/sad.*

Introducing the Book

Say: *This is a book about dogs. On each two-page spread, we see two dogs that are the opposite of each other in some way.* Talk through the book by modeling the form of each sentence. You might say: *What do you see on this page? Yes. This is a big dog.*

Reading the Book

As children read independently, listen to each child read small sections of the text and observe reading behaviors for ways to focus your guidance.

Selecting a Focus

Choose the role of the reader, from the *Kids As* menu, that meets the needs of this reading group. Later, you might return to this book to explore another reader's role.

CHECK THIS

Observe for evidence that children read fluently. Remind them to reread the text, if necessary, to promote comprehension.

LITERACY CENTERS

Writing/Communication Center

Invite children to contribute to a class big book about pets. Have each child draw a picture of a pet and write a sentence describing it. Bind the final pages into a book, and use the book with the whole class.

ABC/Word Center

Randomly display high-frequency words and words that begin with /d/ on cards in a pocket chart. Provide a stack of blank word cards. Invite children to work together writing sentences or a story, using the word cards. Encourage children to take turns reading their work aloud.

KIDS AS...

Meaning Makers Use questions like these to explore with children their role as meaning makers, who gather the book's basic message from print and pictures.

◆ *How are all the dogs in this book the same? How are they different?*

◆ *What words would you use to describe the boy's dog?*

Code Breakers Discuss the elements found in this book to explore with children their role as code breakers, who investigate print to confirm meaning.

Vocabulary	*Writing Conventions*
Word families:	Punctuation:
dog—bog, fog, jog, log	capital letters and periods
Opposites:	Grammar:
big/little, sad/happy	placement of adjectives
	before nouns—*big* dog,
Sounds and Letters	*happy* dog
Hearing sounds:	
/d/—dog	

Text Users Use questions like these to help children explore how genre affects the information, the format, and the purpose of a book.

◆ *What does this book help you learn about dogs?*

◆ *What does it help you learn about opposite words?*

Text Critics Use questions like these to explore how well the author and photographer's work has met the book's purpose.

◆ *What does the author want you to know about dogs? Do you think that message is important?*

◆ *What other characteristics of dogs might the author have chosen to write about?*

duck   dip
dog   dear

LITERACY CENTERS

Interactive Literacy Center
Have a small group of children play *Opposite Charades*. Explain that a child from the group should choose a pair of opposite words and act them out silently for the rest of the group. Challenge the group to guess the actor's word pair. Encourage children to list on chart paper the opposite words they used in the game.

Book Browsing Center
Have children in pairs find two books that someone who likes the book *Dogs* might like. Choices might include books about pets, books about opposites, or books with photographs. Invite the pairs to discuss how their books are similar to the book *Dogs*.

Playing

Children might remember Fay as the child in the *AlphaKids Alphabet Book* for F.

Text Features

- This book explores the things a little girl likes to do when she is playing.
- Simple, repetitive text
- One line of text per page with no return sweep
- Introduces sentence form *I like to _____.*
- Text supported by color photos
- Text placed consistently on page

High-Frequency Words

I, like, to, my, of, all

Getting Ready for Reading

Talk about and list the kinds of activities children like to do when they are outside. Have volunteers describe their favorite outdoor activity using the form *I like to _____.* List the responses on a chart. Display the chart in the *Writing/Communication Center.*

Introducing the Book

You might say: *In this book, Fay tells us what she likes to do when she is playing outside.* Talk through the book, inviting children to help you identify all actions taking place. For some readers, you may wish to point out the change in sentence form on the last page.

Reading the Book

As children read independently, listen to each child read small sections of the text and observe reading behaviors for ways to focus your guidance.

Selecting a Focus

Choose the role of the reader, from the *Kids As* menu, that meets the needs of this reading group. Later, you might return to this book to explore another reader's role.

CHECK THIS

Observe children's ability to read unknown words by using prompts such as *Would _____ fit there?* If children make substitutions, have them reread to the point of error and sound out the first letter of the unknown word with them.

LITERACY CENTERS

Writing/Communication Center

Have children innovate on the text, using the sentence form *I like to _____.* They might write about what they like to do in the classroom or out on the playground. Provide lists of activity words supported by pictures: *read, write, draw, sing, count, talk,* and so on.

ABC/Word Center

Hang action words, such as *run, hide, glide, slide, fall,* on word cards at the center. Invite children to illustrate their favorite action word. Challenge them to hang their picture below the matching action word.

KIDS AS...

Meaning Makers Use questions like these to explore with children their role as meaning makers, who gather the book's basic message from print and pictures.

◆ *What is this book about?*
◆ *What are some of the things Fay likes to do outdoors?*
◆ *Why does Fay like her bath best of all?*

Code Breakers Discuss the elements found in this book to explore with children their role as code breakers, who investigate print to confirm meaning.

Vocabulary
Word families:
run—bun, fun, pun, sun
hide—glide, slide, side, wide
all—ball, call, fall, hall, tall, wall

Writing Conventions
Punctuation:
capital letters, periods, and exclamation points

Sounds and Letters
Hearing sounds:
/l/—like, play, slide

Text Users Use questions like these to help children explore how genre affects the information, the format, and the purpose of a book.

◆ *What does the book help you to learn about?*
◆ *Why has the author put the things Fay does in the order that they appear? Does the order matter?*

Text Critics Use questions like these to explore how well the author and photographer's work has met the book's purpose.

◆ *What does the author think about playing?*
◆ *What does the author think about how playing makes children feel? How can you tell?*

I like to dance.
I like to draw.
I like to play.

LITERACY CENTERS

Interactive Literacy Center
Suggest that children in pairs read the text as a rap song. Invite them to record their song on tape to play to the class. Have children practice the rap inside, using an inside voice. Then, have them practice the rap outside, using their outside voice. Discuss why it is appropriate to change the volume of the voice in certain situations.

Book Browsing Center
Have children find one book showing a child's activity and one book showing an adult's activity. Tell them to talk with a friend about how the child's activity is similar and different from the adult's activity.

My Baby Sister

Children might remember Nina, in this book, as the child in the *AlphaKids Alphabet Book for N.*

Getting Ready for Reading

Talk about babies children know. Ask: *What things can babies do? How do they do them?* You might have children make a list with your help.

Introducing the Book

You might say: *This is a book about Nina's baby sister. It is written as if Nina is talking to us. Her baby sister is learning to do many things just as Nina is. Nina's baby sister likes to do things with her older sister.* As you turn the pages, model the form of the text by saying: *What is the baby sister doing here? Yes. Nina says, "My baby sister likes to read. She likes to read with me."*

Reading the Book

As children read independently, listen to each child read small sections of the text and observe reading behaviors for ways to focus your guidance.

Selecting a Focus

Choose the role of the reader, from the *Kids As* menu, that meets the needs of this reading group. Later, you might return to this book to explore another reader's role.

Text Features

- This book explores the things a baby can do.
- Simple, repetitive text
- One to two lines of text per page with return sweep
- Introduces sentence forms *My baby sister can _____.* and *She can _____ with me.*
- Text supported by color photos
- Text placed consistently on page

High-Frequency Words

This, is, my, can, with, me

CHECK THIS

Observe for evidence regarding directionality with a return sweep. Ask children: *Where does the writing start? Which way does it go? Where does the writing go after that?*

LITERACY CENTERS

Writing/Communication Center

Have children write a list of suggestions to Nina called *Things to Do With a Sister or Brother.* Activities might include *play catch, ride bikes,* or *watch television.* Later, have children write Nina a letter. Invite children to read their class letters and lists aloud.

ABC/Word Center

Encourage children to explore the initial sound /s/. Provide magazines, glue, and butcher paper to make an /s/ mural. Invite children to look in magazines and brochures to find pictures of things with the initial sound /s/. Have them cut out and paste the pictures onto the mural.

KIDS AS...

Meaning Makers Use questions like these to explore with children their role as meaning makers, who gather the book's basic message from print and pictures.

- *What can Nina's baby sister do?*
- *Which things does the baby need help to do?*
- *How do you think Nina feels about her baby sister?*

Code Breakers Discuss the elements found in this book to explore with children their role as code breakers, who investigate print to confirm meaning.

Vocabulary
Word families:
can—man, ran, Dan, fan, plan

Sounds and Letters
Hearing sounds:
/s/—sister, see

Writing Conventions
Punctuation:
capital letters and periods
Grammar:
pronouns—me, my
question words—Can

Text Users Use questions like these to help children explore how genre affects the information, the format, and the purpose of a book.

- *What message do you think the author is trying to share about having a baby sister?*
- *How might this book help a friend who has a younger brother or sister?*

Text Critics Use questions like these to explore how well the author and photographer's work has met the book's purpose.

- *Do you find this book interesting? Why do think so?*
- *How would the book be different if the baby's father told the story to us?*

LITERACY CENTERS

Book Browsing Center
Provide books that have children as the main characters. Have children choose books about a boy or girl they might want as a sibling. Invite them to tell a friend the reasons for their choice.

Interactive Literacy Center
Provide a blank cassette tape. Suggest that, on the tape, children record messages sharing what they like about baby sisters or brothers. Later listen to and discuss the tape together. You may want to write their comments on chart paper as you discuss them.

Grandpa's House

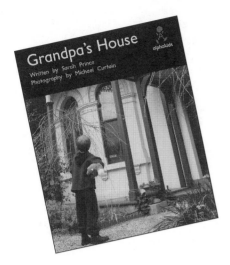

Text Features

- This book explores the idea that, when you are young, things around you can seem very big.
- Simple, repetitive text
- Two lines of text with a return sweep
- Introduces sentence form *Grandpa has a house with a very big _____.*
- Text supported by color photos
- Text placed consistently on page

High-Frequency Words

has, a, with, big

Getting Ready for Reading

Talk about times when children feel small. For example, they might feel small in a crowd at a busy shopping mall. Talk about familiar childhood experiences, such as being unable to reach things around the house. Look at photographs of big buildings, and talk about how you would feel, as a child, if you were visiting this building.

Introducing the Book

You might say:

This is a book about a little boy who is going to visit his grandpa and spend the night. His grandpa lives in a very big house with very big things in it. It has a very big yard, a very big door, a very big hall, a flight of very big stairs, and a very big bed.

Reading the Book

As children read independently, listen to each child read small sections of the text and observe reading behaviors for ways to focus your guidance.

Selecting a Focus

Choose the role of the reader, from the *Kids As* menu, that meets the needs of this reading group. Later, you might return to this book to explore another reader's role.

CHECK THIS

Observe for evidence that children use cues that show they know how to problem solve. Say: *Try hall. What word would make sense? Now, try very. Would that word make sense?*

LITERACY CENTERS

Writing/Communication Center

Have children write about a big place that they visit. Provide a list of family member words, words that name objects found around the home, and other words naming things children might encounter on a visit to that place.

ABC/Word Center

Challenge children to create a nonsense poem using the word families of *Grandpa's House*. Use the sentence form:
Grandpa has a house with a very big (word rhyming with big).
Grandpa has a house with a very tall (word rhyming with tall).

KIDS AS...

Meaning Makers Use questions like these to explore with children their role as meaning makers, who gather the book's basic message from print and pictures.

- ◆ *What big things does Grandpa's house have?*
- ◆ *Why does the little boy like going to Grandpa's house?*

Code Breakers Discuss the elements found in this book to explore with children their role as code breakers, who investigate print to confirm meaning.

Vocabulary
Word families:
big—dig, fig, jig, pig, wig
hall—all, ball, call, fall, tall

Sounds and Letters
Hearing sounds:
/g/—Grandpa, Good night
/h/—house, has, hall
short /a/—Grandpa, has

Hearing words:
Children clap for each word in a sentence.

Writing Conventions
Punctuation:
capital letters, periods, and possessives
Grammar:
change of form
from: ___ *with a very big*
to: ___ *with very big*

Text Users Use questions like these to help children explore how genre affects the information, the format, and the purpose of a book.

- ◆ *What type of book is this—fiction or factual?*
- ◆ *Why do you think the author used photographs instead of drawings?*

Text Critics Use questions like these to explore how well the author and photographer's work has met the book's purpose.

- ◆ *What did you like about this book?*
- ◆ *Is the book more interesting with photographs instead of drawings? Why do you think so?*

Grandpa has a house with a very big pig.

LITERACY CENTERS

Interactive Literacy Center
Have children listen to a cassette tape of *Too Much Noise* by Ann McGovern. Encourage children to retell the story in a drawing. Challenge them to remember the order in which the animals created the noises in the old man's home. Include a copy of the book, *Too Much Noise*, in the center for further reference.

Book Browsing Center
Have children find a book about a place they like to visit or would like to visit, do not like to visit, or do not mind visiting when they have to. Suggest children write their place on a class list. Later, you may wish to discuss the list with the class.

I'm Brave

Text Features

- This book is about a young girl overcoming her fears about catching the school bus by imagining she is brave enough to catch fierce creatures.
- Simple, repetitive text
- Three lines of text with a return sweep
- Introduces sentence *I'm brave.* and the sentence form *I can catch a ____.*
- Text supported by color illustrations
- Text placed consistently on page

High-Frequency Words

I'm, I, can, a

Getting Ready for Reading

Talk about times when children have felt scared about doing something. Ask children: *How have you talked yourself into being brave and doing the thing that frightened you?*

Introducing the Book

You might say: *This is a book about a little girl who says she is brave.* Talk through the book, identifying the real and make-believe creatures the girl faces: *What has the little girl been brave enough to catch here? Yes. The girl is telling us "I'm brave. I can catch a lion."* As you talk, ensure that children can name each animal in the book.

Reading the Book

As children read independently, listen to each child read small sections of the text and observe reading behaviors for ways to focus your guidance.

Selecting a Focus

Choose the role of the reader, from the *Kids As* menu, that meets the needs of this reading group. Later, you might return to this book to explore another reader's role.

CHECK THIS

Observe for evidence that children look at the pictures to find useful information when reading the text. You might say: *Look at the picture. What word would make sense by looking at the picture?*

LITERACY CENTERS

Writing/Communication Center

Have children write about times when they needed to be brave to do something. Suggest a story starter, such as *I had to be brave when I had to ____.*

ABC/Word Center

Have children make pairs of cards using high-frequency words from *I'm Brave* and such words from earlier *AlphaKids Guided Readers*. Then invite them to use the words in a game of Concentration to build their sight word skills.

KIDS AS...

Meaning Makers Use questions like these to explore with children their role as meaning makers, who gather the book's basic message from print and pictures.

- *Where in the story did you learn how she catches the tiger?*
- *How does the girl really feel about catching the bus? How can you tell?*
- *Why does the girl say she is brave enough to catch all the creatures that she names?*

Code Breakers Discuss the elements found in this book to explore with children their role as code breakers, who investigate print to confirm meaning.

Vocabulary
Word awareness:
contractions—I'm/I am
Word families:
can—ban, Dan, fan, man, pan, ran, van

Sounds and Letters
Hearing sounds:
/c/—can, catch

Writing Conventions
Punctuation:
capital letters and periods
Grammar:
a and *the* before nouns

Text Users Use questions like these to help children explore how genre affects the information, the format, and the purpose of a book.

- *Would most people read this book for fun or for information? Why do you think so?*

Text Critics Use questions like these to explore how well the author and illustrator's work has met the book's purpose.

- *What does the author want us to know about being afraid? Do you agree with the author's message? Why?*

LITERACY CENTERS

Interactive Literacy Center
On cassette or videotape, have children interview a partner about a time when their partner had to be brave. Provide a list of sample questions in the center: (1) Have you ever had to be brave? (2) When did you act bravely? (3) How old were you? (4) Why did you act bravely? Include items such as empty paper towel rolls for children who might wish to use pretend microphones for the interview.

Book Browsing Center
Motivate children to do character studies. Have them each find a book about a character he or she thinks is brave. Suggest that children honor their character in a poster, to be hung in the center. Provide crayons, poster board, and creative art materials to decorate the poster.

Living and Nonliving

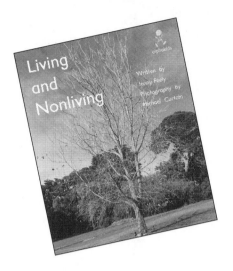

Text Features

- This book is an information text comparing living and nonliving things.
- Simple, repetitive text
- One line of text with no return sweep
- Introduces sentence forms: _____ are living. _____ are nonliving.
- Text supported by color photos
- Text placed consistently on page

High-Frequency Words

are

Getting Ready for Reading

Discuss the difference between living and nonliving things, then record children's responses on chart paper. Ask children to name examples of living and nonliving things in the classroom as well as just outside the classroom walls.

Introducing the Book

Talk through the book. You might say: *This is a book that groups things as living and nonliving.* Showing children the first page, ensure that they can identify the focus of the pages of the book. Ask: *What is this a picture of? Is it living or nonliving?* Model the sentence form: *Yes. Trees are living.* Remind children that pictures provide clues to identify words they do not know.

Reading the Book

As children read independently, listen to each child read small sections of the text and observe reading behaviors for ways to focus your guidance.

Selecting a Focus

Choose the role of the reader, from the *Kids As* menu, that meets the needs of this reading group. Later, you might return to this book to explore another reader's role.

CHECK THIS

Observe for evidence that children are able to read new words by using known words or concepts. As a miscue strategy, you might ask: *Does that word make sense? Does that word sound right? Does that word look right?*

LITERACY CENTERS

Writing/Communication Center

Have children write and illustrate new pages for their own book, *Living and Nonliving*. Remind them to use the sentence forms ___ are living. ___ are nonliving. Provide a picture dictionary as a word source.

ABC/Word Center

Make a mobile classifying living and nonliving things. At the top, hang the heading, *All Things*. Hang two subheads, *Living* and *Nonliving*, below. Provide children with magazine pictures. Encourage children to group the pictures as *Living* or *Nonliving*. Then attach the pictures below the appropriate subheads on the mobile.

KIDS AS...

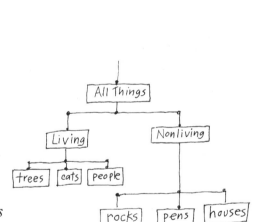

Meaning Makers Use questions like these to explore with children their role as meaning makers, who gather the book's basic message from print and pictures.

- *Which things in the book are living?*
- *Which things are nonliving?*

Code Breakers Discuss the elements found in this book to explore with children their role as code breakers, who investigate print to confirm meaning.

Vocabulary

plural nouns—animals, rocks, trees, fires, birds, metals, fish, rivers, people, houses

bring—ring, sing, wing
fish—wish, dish

Sounds and Letters
Hearing sounds:
/ing/—living

Writing Conventions
Punctuation:
capital letters and periods
Grammar:
are with plural nouns

Text Users Use questions like these to help children explore how genre affects the information, the format, and the purpose of a book.

- *What could someone learn by reading this book?*
- *What might you use page 12 to help you do?*

Text Critics Use questions like these to explore how well the author and photographer's work has met the book's purpose.

- *Why do you think the author has put people and houses on facing pages? Was that a good idea?*
- *Is the book easier to understand because it has photographs instead of drawings? Why do you think so?*

LITERACY CENTERS

Interactive Literacy Center
Challenge children to attach labels that read *Living* and *Nonliving* to items in the classroom. Remind children that any child's name they see can be considered a part of the room. Ask: *Would a member of the class be living or nonliving?*

Book Browsing Center
Include books about living and nonliving things, such as *Ocean Day* by Shelly Rotner, *Everything Grows* by Raffi, and *Trucks* by Anne Rockwell. Encourage children to identify which objects in the books are living and which are nonliving. You may want to record their findings on chart paper.

What's This? What's That?

Text Features

- This book is a rhyming guessing game.
- Simple, repetitive text
- One line of text in a question-and-answer pattern
- Introduces sentences *What's this? What's that?* and the phrase *a _____ on a _____.*
- Text supported by color illustrations
- Text placed consistently on page

High-Frequency Words

what's, this, that, a, on, in

Getting Ready for Reading

Before class meets, trace the outline of a pair of scissors, a flat button, and a dollar bill onto a sheet of paper. Invite children to guess what objects you might have used to make each tracing. After children have finished guessing, produce a collection of small objects that includes the three items you used to make the tracings. Ask volunteers to identify the object that matches each outline and encourage them to explain how they determined the matching object. Place the collection of objects in the *Interactive Literacy Center* for a follow-up activity.

Introducing the Book

Say: *This book is like a guessing game.* Turn to page 3. Have children guess what the blue object is. Model the form of the text. Point to the hat brim and say: *What's this?* Point to the hat crown and say: *What's that?*

Reading the Book

As children read independently, listen to each child read small sections of the text and observe reading behaviors for ways to focus your guidance.

Selecting a Focus

Choose the role of the reader, from the *Kids As* menu, that meets the needs of this reading group. Later, you might return to this book to explore another reader's role.

CHECK THIS

Observe for evidence that children understand punctuation. Ask them to locate the punctuation in the text: *Can you point to a question mark? Why do we have a question mark here?*

LITERACY CENTERS

Writing/Communication Center

Provide glue and construction paper. Have children trace any shape. Then challenge children to fill in that shape with something new the shape might represent. Suggest they caption their picture, using the phrase *a _____ on a _____;* or *a _____ in a _____.*

ABC/Word Center

Write high-frequency words and -og and -at words on word cards. Randomly place the cards in a pocket chart. Invite children to sort word cards by using the questions *How are the words alike? How are the words different?* Challenge children to write sentences with the words.

KIDS AS...

Meaning Makers Use questions like these to explore with children their role as meaning makers, who gather the book's basic message from print and pictures.

♦ *What did you think the bear on the chair would be?*
♦ *If you added two pages to the book, what would they be?*

Code Breakers Discuss the elements found in this book to explore with children their role as code breakers, who investigate print to confirm meaning.

Vocabulary
Word families:
cat—bat, fat, mat, pat, rat, sat
frog—bog, dog, fog, hog, jog, log
Rhyming words:
cat/mat, frog/log, mouse/house, bear/chair

Writing Conventions
Punctuation:
capital letters, periods, question marks, and apostrophes
Grammar:
contractions—what's/what is

Sounds and Letters
Hearing sounds:
/at/—cat, hat, that, mat, rat

Text Users Use questions like these to help children explore how genre affects the information, the format, and the purpose of a book.

♦ *How is this book different from a storybook?*
♦ *What did the author need to do to write this book?*

Text Critics Use questions like these to explore how well the author and illustrator's work has met the book's purpose.

♦ *Why has the author chosen to use the pattern* What's This? What's That? *Was that a good idea?*
♦ *Would this book make sense if there were no illustrations?*

LITERACY CENTERS

Interactive Literacy Center
Provide several small objects with interesting shapes. Have pairs of children play a guessing game. Suggest that the first child pick an object and trace around it on paper while the second child looks elsewhere. Challenge the second child to guess which object was traced. Include *It Looked Like Spilt Milk* by Charles Shaw and have the two children take turns reading it to each other.

Book Browsing Center
Provide children with familiar poems and rhymes to read with a partner. Have the pairs work cooperatively to compile a list of rhyming words. They might share their lists with the entire class or make a rhyming book of their own.

Sandwiches

Text Features

- This book is about the sandwiches a boy had during each day of the week.
- Simple, repetitive text
- Three lines of text with two return sweeps
- Introduces sentence form *I had a _____ sandwich for my lunch on _____.* The last page introduces a change to the sentence form.
- Text supported by color illustrations
- Text placed consistently on page

High-Frequency Words

I, had, a, for, my, on, dad

Getting Ready for Reading

Discuss with children sandwiches they might have for lunch today. Invite them to help you list sandwich fillings they like best. Ask: *Who might usually make these sandwiches? What would you make if you could make the weirdest sandwich you can think of?*

Introducing the Book

Say: *This is a book about the sandwiches that a boy had each day of the week. During the week his dad made the sandwiches, but on Saturday the boy made a sandwich for his dad.* Talk through the book looking at the sandwiches the boy had each day. Say: *What sandwich did the boy have on Monday? Yes, it looks like he had a cheese sandwich on Monday.* Repeat for each sandwich type. Draw children's attention to the change in text structure on page 12.

Reading the Book

As children read independently, listen to each child read small sections of the text and observe reading behaviors for ways to focus your guidance.

Selecting a Focus

Choose the role of the reader, from the *Kids As* menu, that meets the needs of this reading group. Later, you might return to this book to explore another reader's role.

CHECK THIS

Observe for evidence that children read fluently. Uncover one line at a time and say: *Read this line. Can you read it so that it sounds like people talk?*

LITERACY CENTERS

Writing/Communication Center

Provide construction paper, glue, and recyclable scraps. Have partners create the weirdest sandwich they can think of. Allow partners to swap sandwiches and each finish the sentence forms *I had a _____ sandwich. (Name of the partner) made this sandwich for me.*

ABC/Word Center

Write the days of the week on word cards. Cut each word into syllables. Encourage children to connect pieces to form a day of the week. Invite them to arrange the days of the week on the floor in the proper sequence.

AlphaKids Guided Readers

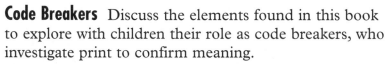

Meaning Makers Use questions like these to explore with children their role as meaning makers, who gather the book's basic message from print and pictures.

◆ *What sandwiches did the boy have? Who made them?*

◆ *Do the boy and his dad like the sandwiches? How can you tell?*

Code Breakers Discuss the elements found in this book to explore with children their role as code breakers, who investigate print to confirm meaning.

Vocabulary
Day words:
Monday, Tuesday, Wednesday, Thursday, Friday, Saturday, birthday

Sounds and Letters
Hearing sounds:
/ch/—cheese, chicken, sandwich

Writing Conventions
Punctuation:
capital letters—for days of the week
periods
Grammar:
a and *the* before nouns

Text Users Use questions like these to help children explore how genre affects the information, the format, and the purpose of a book.

◆ *Does this book teach you how to make a sandwich? How would a book that teaches you how to make a sandwich be different?*

Text Critics Use questions like these to explore how well the author and illustrator's work has met the book's purpose.

◆ *Why do you think the author has the boy make the sandwich on Saturday?*

◆ *Does the ending make the book better? Why do you think so?*

LITERACY CENTERS

Interactive Literacy Center
Display a *how-to-make* picture of any food familiar to children, such as a pizza, for reference. Have children draw the steps necessary to make a sandwich. Provide poster board and markers as well as sandwich words, such as *bread, chicken, cheese, ham, peanut butter,* and *jelly*. Later, suggest that children demonstrate how to make their sandwiches to the class.

Book Browsing Center
Motivate children to search for books about food or go to earlier *AlphaKids Guided Reader* books such as *Ice Cream* and *Fruit Salad*. Invite them to tell a friend which foods they could happily eat every day of the year and which foods they wish would disappear forever.

What's for Dinner?

Text Features

- This book is a chant. The last page reveals the joke.
- Repetitive text
- One line of text with no return sweep
- Introduces sentence form *The _____ asked the _____.*
- Text supported by color illustrations
- Text placed consistently on page

High-Frequency Words

the, for, asked

Getting Ready for Reading

Model the form of the text. Provide each child with a card showing the name and picture of an animal in the book. Have children take turns asking each other *What's for dinner?* pretending to be the animal on their card. One child then retells the entire game from memory: *The lion asked the tiger, the tiger asked the bat . . .*

Introducing the Book

You might say: *This is a book in which animals ask each other "What's for dinner?"* Talk through the book, focusing on animal names by saying: *Who asked "What's for dinner?" here? Yes. The lion asked the tiger.* You might point out that in the illustrations the animal doing the asking is always to the left of the animal being asked.

Reading the Book

As children read independently, listen to each child read small sections of the text and observe reading behaviors for ways to focus your guidance.

Selecting a Focus

Choose the role of the reader, from the *Kids As* menu, that meets the needs of this reading group. Later, you might return to this book to explore another reader's role.

CHECK THIS

Observe for evidence that children check their predictions. For example, if the child says *bat* instead of *tiger,* a prompt could be: *Check the beginning letter of the word.*

LITERACY CENTERS

Writing/Communication Center

Have children think about what foods a rabbit might eat. Provide a sample menu on poster board for children to refer to. Challenge them to create a menu for a rabbit. You might display their menus in the *Book Browsing Center.*

ABC/Word Center

Invite pairs of children to play *Memory.* Use the *Code Breaker* list of *-at* words to make two sets of nine word cards. Have them shuffle the cards and lay them face down. Have partners take turns flipping two cards face up to find a match. The winner has the most matching word cards.

KIDS AS...

Meaning Makers Use questions like these to explore with children their role as meaning makers, who gather the book's basic message from print and pictures.

- *What did each animal want for dinner?*
- *Why do you think the rabbit jumped down the hole?*

Code Breakers Discuss the elements found in this book to explore with children their role as code breakers, who investigate print to confirm meaning.

Vocabulary
Word families:
cat—bat, fat, flat, mat, pat, rat, sat, that

Sounds and Letters
Hearing words:
Children clap for each syllable in words:

    ★ ★   ★
    li-on   bat

Hearing sounds:
medial short /a/ sound—
bat, cat, rabbit

Writing Conventions
Punctuation:
capital letters, periods, and question marks
Grammar:
word ending—ed

Text Users Use questions like these to help children explore how genre affects the information, the format, and the purpose of a book.

- *How could you tell which animal would talk next?*
- *Is this story real or make-believe? How can you tell?*

Text Critics Use questions like these to explore how well the author and illustrator's work has met the book's purpose.

- *Did the author do a good job? What would you have the animals say if they could talk?*
- *How can you tell if the author knows what these animals eat?*

LITERACY CENTERS

Interactive Literacy Center
Have children use paper plates, construction paper, and elastic to make a mask of an animal in a zoo. Challenge them to wear their mask, act like that animal, and give it a voice. Suggest that children use their masks and put on a skit about animals at the zoo asking the zookeeper, *"What's for dinner?"* Allow children to perform their skit later for the class.

Book Browsing Center
Provide encyclopedias for browsing. Suggest that children search for pictures of animals of different sizes. Have children talk to a friend about what they think each animal might eat. Later, you might help children draw up a list showing the animals they found.

Monsters

Text Features

- This is a book about children in monster costumes that do particular things.
- Repetitive text
- Two lines of text with a return sweep
- Introduces sentence form *I have big ___ to ___ everything*. The form changes at the end.
- Text supported by color illustrations
- Text placed consistently on page

High-Frequency Words

I, have, big, to, see, a, am, get, you

Getting Ready for Reading

Discuss what a monster is. Talk about times children have made masks or dressed up as monsters. What did they use to make themselves look like monsters? How did they speak to others when they were wearing their masks?

Introducing the Book

You might say: *This is a book about children who make themselves into monsters. They use props to help them do particular things.* Talk through the book, saying things like: *This child has made big eyes so that she can see everything. This child has made big ears to hear everything.*

Reading the Book

As children read independently, listen to each child read small sections of the text and observe reading behaviors for ways to focus your guidance.

Selecting a Focus

Choose the role of the reader, from the *Kids As* menu, that meets the needs of this reading group. Later, you might return to this book to explore another reader's role.

CHECK THIS

Observe for evidence that children monitor their own reading. If children pause at an unknown word, some prompts to encourage them might be: *What do you notice about the word? What words do you know that might help you figure this one out?*

LITERACY CENTERS

Writing/Communication Center
Post the sentence form *I have big ___ to ___ everything*. Have children draw cartoon characters with one outrageous feature. Suggest that they draw and write what the silly feature might do. Have them attach the sentence to their cartoon.

ABC/Word Center
Have pairs of children read the room to find and list compound words, or suggest that they generate their own lists. Provide a chart to allow children to record the compound words from their lists. You might read the chart with the class later.

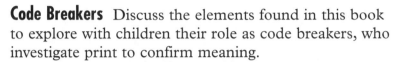

Meaning Makers Use questions like these to explore with children their role as meaning makers, who gather the book's basic message from print and pictures.

♦ *What does the child say her big ears will do?*
♦ *Why have the children dressed as monsters?*

Code Breakers Discuss the elements found in this book to explore with children their role as code breakers, who investigate print to confirm meaning.

Vocabulary
Word families:
big—dig, pig, wig, jig
see—bee, knee
get—bet, let, met, net, pet, set, vet, yet

Sounds and Letters
Hearing sounds:
medial short /i/—big, everything

Writing Conventions
Punctuation:
capital letters, periods, and exclamation marks
Grammar:
compound words—every/thing

Text Users Use questions like these to help children explore how genre affects the information, the format, and the purpose of a book.

♦ *Where does the book end? Why do you think the author used a different kind of sentence at the end?*

Text Critics Use questions like these to explore how well the author and illustrator's work has met the book's purpose.

♦ *Does the illustrator's work make the book better? Why?*
♦ *Where might the author have heard:* I have big ____ to ____ everything?

LITERACY CENTERS

Interactive Literacy Center
Make a Venn diagram. Label the outside circle sections *Monsters* and *Little Red Riding Hood* and the interconnecting section *Monsters AND Little Red Riding Hood*. Then have children read *Little Red Riding Hood* and write the differences between the books in the sections with only that book's name, while they write similarities in the section where the circles overlap.

Book Browsing Center
Provide books about monsters. Suggest that children tell a friend which books they like most and which they like least. Have them write their favorite titles on a class *My Favorite Books* chart to use when selecting books.

The Party

Text Features

- This book explores a girl's experiences at her birthday party.
- Repetitive text
- Three lines of text with two return sweeps.
- Introduces sentence form *I'm having a party with lots of _____ and lots of _____.*
- Text supported by color illustrations
- Text placed consistently on page

High-Frequency Words

I'm, a, with, of, and

Getting Ready for Reading

Ask children to talk about parties they have been to. Ask: *What things did you see there?* List children's answers, grouping them by initial letter. Your list might include, for example, *cake* and *candles* or *presents* and *people.*

Introducing the Book

Talk through the book by saying: *This is a book about a girl's birthday party and the things she had at it.* Turn to each page, pointing out things at her party, such as *balloons, hats, candles, ice cream, games, friends,* and *presents.*

Reading the Book

As children read independently, listen to each child read small sections of the text and observe reading behaviors for ways to focus your guidance.

Selecting a Focus

Choose the role of the reader, from the *Kids As* menu, that meets the needs of this reading group. Later, you might return to this book to explore another reader's role.

CHECK THIS

Observe for evidence that children predict what would make sense as they read. A prompt to promote this might include: *What might you say that would make sense? Would* balloon *fit here? Do you think this word might look like the word* balloon?

LITERACY CENTERS

Writing/Communication Center

Challenge children to imagine they were guests at the girl's party. Provide an example of a thank-you note and have children write a thank-you note to the girl. As a writing prompt, display the children's list made in *Getting Ready for Reading.*

ABC/Word Center

Provide several blank word cards and two cards that read -*at* and -*ake.* Have children write an initial sound on a blank card that together with one of the rimes builds a word. Include a chart in the center on which children can write the words they build.

KIDS AS...

Meaning Makers Use questions like these to explore with children their role as meaning makers, who gather the book's basic message from print and pictures.

- *What in the words and pictures shows this is a party?*
- *Which part of the party was most important to the girl? How can you tell?*

Code Breakers Discuss the elements found in this book to explore with children their role as code breakers, who investigate print to confirm meaning.

Vocabulary
Seeing words within words:
balloon—ball, party—part, candles—can
Word families:
hat—bat, sat, fat, mat, flat, cat, rat, that, pat
cake—make, take, lake, rake, bake

Sounds and Letters
Hearing sounds:
/p/—party, presents
/c/—cake, candles

Writing Conventions
Punctuation:
periods, ellipses
Grammar:
singular and plural—balloon/s, hat/s, candle/s, game/s, cake/s, present/s
contractions—I'm/I am

Text Users Use questions like these to help children explore how genre affects the information, the format, and the purpose of a book.

- *What clues show that everyone enjoyed the party?*
- *How would this story be different if an adult had the party?*

Text Critics Use questions like these to explore how well the author and illustrator's work has met the book's purpose.

- *Is this party like a real party? How?*
- *Do you think the author knows why parties are fun?*

I'm having a party with lots of games.

LITERACY CENTERS

Interactive Literacy Center
Provide construction paper and glue, and encourage children to make invitations to a party. Post the sentence form *I'm having a party with lots of ____.* on a chart. Suggest that children write what they would like to have lots of at a party. Have children glue the sentence to a construction paper card and then decorate the card to make it more inviting.

Book Browsing Center
Provide books about celebrations around the world and books about an event with "lots of something." Suggest that children discuss their book with a friend to decide which celebrations might be easiest to plan and gather party supplies for.

Too Busy

Text Features

- This book is about two children and their busy parent.
- Repetitive text
- Two lines of text with a return sweep
- Introduces sentence form *Can we go play _____?* and the response *Not now. I'm too busy.* The form changes on last two pages.
- Text supported by color illustrations
- Text placed in speech bubbles

High-Frequency Words

Can, we, go, play, Not, now, I'm, too

Getting Ready for Reading

Discuss times when children have wanted their parent or caretaker's attention but were told that the parent or caretaker was too busy. Ask children to share how that response made them feel. You might discuss positive responses they could make to the situation.

Introducing the Book

Talk through the book by saying: *This is a book about two children who want their mom to play with them, but she is always too busy.* Turn to the first page of the book and say: *What game do the kids want to play? What do you think their mom will say?* Continue paging through the book, discussing other activities the children propose. At the end, you might say: *What do you think the kids finally decided to do?*

Reading the Book

As children read independently, listen to each child read small sections of the text and observe reading behaviors for ways to focus your guidance.

Selecting a Focus

Choose the role of the reader, from the *Kids As* menu, that meets the needs of this reading group. Later, you might return to this book to explore another reader's role.

CHECK THIS

Draw children's attention to speech balloons and point out how the speech balloon is drawn to show who is speaking. Ask children to read the text as if they were the character who is talking.

LITERACY CENTERS

Writing/Communication Center
Provide a large sheet of paper entitled *Advice. What might you do?* Encourage children to write advice that might help the two children in the book share their feelings with their mother or help the family spend time together.

ABC/Word Center
Provide word cards with a contraction on one side and the two words the contraction represents on the other side. Have one child flash a card to another child and challenge him or her to respond with the parts the word is made up of. Have partners reverse the task and their roles.

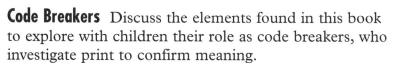 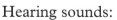
KIDS AS...

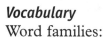

Meaning Makers Use questions like these to explore with children their role as meaning makers, who gather the book's basic message from print and pictures.

- *Was the children's mother really too busy? Were the children really too busy? How can you tell?*

Code Breakers Discuss the elements found in this book to explore with children their role as code breakers, who investigate print to confirm meaning.

Vocabulary
Word families:
play—clay, day, hay, lay, may, pay, say, way
now—bow, cow, how, shower, flower

Sounds and Letters
Hearing words:
Children lay out a counter for every syllable they hear in a word.

Hearing sounds:
/b/—basketball
/ee/ sound of *y*: busy

Writing Conventions
Punctuation:
question marks, exclamation marks, and apostrophes
Grammar:
question words —Can
contractions—I'm/I am

Text Users Use questions like these to help children explore how genre affects the information, the format, and the purpose of a book.

- *What other books might have speech bubbles? How do speech bubbles change the way you read a book?*

Text Critics Use questions like these to explore how well the author and illustrator's work has met the book's purpose.

- *What do you think the author is saying about families?*
- *How are families you know the same as or different from this family?*

LITERACY CENTERS

Interactive Literacy Center
Suggest that children use speech bubbles in writing an additional scene for *Too Busy*. Have children write what they think the characters might say when they finally play together. Invite children to act out their scene by reading the speech bubbles. Some children might wish to perform for the class.

Book Browsing Center
Provide a shoe box to use as a Suggestion Box. Have children look for books that children from any family might enjoy. Ask children to write the titles on paper and drop the paper in the box. Read the suggestions as a class, choosing read-aloud and read-together books.

The Mailbox

Text Features

- This book explores the items that are likely to arrive in the family mailbox.
- Repetitive text
- One to four lines of text on a page in a question-and-answer pattern
- Variation in sentence form with direct speech
- Text supported by color illustrations
- Text placed consistently on page

High-Frequency Words

the, I, have, from, said, Mom, Dad, is, it, a, no, it's, not, an, for

Getting Ready for Reading

Show children a *bill, card, newspaper, invitation,* and *package* and identify them by name: *This is a bill. This is a card.* Play *What's in the mailbox?* Say: *I have something from the mailbox.* Children try to identify the item by asking: *It's a (bill)?* Answer: *No. It's not a ___.* or *Yes. It's a ___.* The child who guesses correctly gets to guess again.

Introducing the Book

Talk through the book by saying: *This is a book about mail that comes to a family's house. Everyone tries to guess what the mail is.* Turn to each page and point out the thought bubbles that indicate what the speaker thinks and says the mail might be. Discuss the change in sentence form on page 11. You might say: *Now Sam knows what the mail is.*

Reading the Book

As children read independently, listen to each child read small sections of the text and observe reading behaviors for ways to focus your guidance.

Selecting a Focus

Choose the role of the reader, from the *Kids As* menu, that meets the needs of this reading group. Later, you might return to this book to explore another reader's role.

CHECK THIS

Observe for evidence of phrased or fluent reading behaviors that link oral language expression to text. Prompts might be: *Read the sentence as if you are talking. Read the sentence as if you are the person in the story.*

LITERACY CENTERS

Writing/Communication Center

Provide a bag containing mail items that you used during *Getting Ready for Reading.* Invite children to look at and touch each item in the bag. Then have them complete the sentence form *It's a (item of mail).* Confirm their guesses when you meet.

ABC/Word Center

Provide the words *a* and *an* on word cards with adhesive on the back. Display the words *apple, pill, bill, igloo,* and *arm* in a column on a chart. Have children stick the articles that would make sense with a particular word next to that word on the chart.

KIDS AS...

Meaning Makers Use questions like these to explore with children their role as meaning makers, who gather the book's basic message from print and pictures.

- ◆ *What came in the mail? Was Sam pleased to get it?*
- ◆ *Why did each person guess a different type of mail?*

Code Breakers Discuss the elements found in this book to explore with children their role as code breakers, who investigate print to confirm meaning.

Vocabulary
Word families:
not—cot, dot, got, hot
bill—ill, will, kill, fill, mill
an—man, can, Dan, fan
it—bit, fit, hit, lit, pit, sit

Sounds and Letters
Hearing words:
Children clap to indicate syllables in mail words:

bill   mag-a-zine

Hearing sounds:
/i/—it, invitation

Writing Conventions
Punctuation:
question marks, quotation marks, and commas
Grammar:
a and *an* before nouns
contractions—it's/it is

Text Users Use questions like these to help children explore how genre affects the information, the format, and the purpose of a book.

- ◆ *Why do you think the pictures have thought bubbles?*

Text Critics Use questions like these to explore how well the author and illustrator's work has met the book's purpose.

- ◆ *Why do you think the author had Mom play the guessing game?*
- ◆ *Do the thought bubbles make the book easier to understand? Why?*

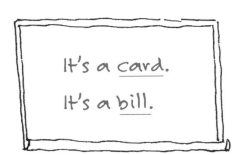

It's a card.
It's a bill.

LITERACY CENTERS

Interactive Literacy Center
Challenge children to use the sentences they wrote at the *Writing/Communication Center* to draw thought bubbles. Encourage them to look at the thought bubbles in *The Mailbox* to get ideas. Invite children to draw themselves below the thought bubbles.

Book Browsing Center
Include books of riddles in the center. Invite children to ask each other riddles. Later, some children might like to ask the class one of their favorite riddles.

Butterfly

Text Features

- This is a factual text that explores the life cycle of a butterfly.
- Repetitive text
- Three lines of text with two return sweeps
- Introduces sentence form *There was a _____ on a leaf*. A diagram is introduced on the last page.
- Text supported by color photos
- Text placed consistently on page

High-Frequency Words

Then, there, was, a, on

Getting Ready for Reading

Ask the children if they have ever seen a butterfly or are familiar with how a caterpillar becomes a butterfly. You might view a video or share a big book about the life cycle of a butterfly. It may be helpful to write *chrysalis* onto a chart and have children practice saying it. Talk about what a chrysalis is.

Introducing the Book

Talk through the book by saying: *This book tells the story of a butterfly. First the butterfly lays an egg on a leaf.* Turn to each page of the book, mentioning the technical nouns, such as *butterfly, egg, leaf, caterpillar,* and *chrysalis.* Say: *This page shows a butterfly on a leaf. This page shows an egg on a leaf,* and so on.

Reading the Book

As children read independently, listen to each child read small sections of the text and observe reading behaviors for ways to focus your guidance.

Selecting a Focus

Choose the role of the reader, from the *Kids As* menu, that meets the needs of this reading group. Later, you might return to this book to explore another reader's role.

CHECK THIS

Observe for evidence that children self-correct as they read. A prompt to encourage this would be: *It was good the way you worked that out.*

LITERACY CENTERS

Writing/Communication Center

Challenge children to create a picture book about the life cycle of a butterfly. Include the words *egg, leaf, caterpillar, chrysalis,* and *butterfly* at the center, along with a copy of *Butterfly.* Have them write and illustrate the changes during the butterfly's life cycle.

ABC/Word Center

Write 3 sentences from *Butterfly* omitting capital letters and punctuation. Provide the book for each child and markers of many colors. Have children add punctuation and capital letters where they belong. You might discuss their results together later.

KIDS AS...

Meaning Makers Use questions like these to explore with children their role as meaning makers, who gather the book's basic message from print and pictures.

- *What is this book about?*
- *What changes happen as the butterfly grows from an egg to a caterpillar? What happens first? last? What will happen after the book ends?*

Code Breakers Discuss the elements found in this book to explore with children their role as code breakers, who investigate print to confirm meaning.

Vocabulary
Seeing words within words:
butterfly—but, butter, fly

Sounds and Letters
Hearing words:
Children raise a finger to represent each word they hear on each page as the text is read aloud.

Hearing sounds:
/b/—butterfly

Writing Conventions
Punctuation:
capital letters and periods
Visual literacy:
reading a chart—direction, labels, and title

Text Users Use questions like these to help children explore how genre affects the information, the format, and the purpose of a book.

- *Is the butterfly at the beginning of the book the same one we see at the end? Does the text on pages 2 and 10 tell you that the butterflies are not the same? How?*

Text Critics Use questions like these to explore how well the author and photographer's work has met the book's purpose.

- *Did the diagram make the book easier or harder to understand? Why?*

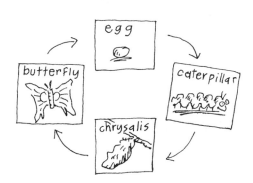

LITERACY CENTERS

Interactive Literacy Center
Have children create time lines of their life on butcher paper. Provide markers and sentence starters as prompts, such as *When I was born . . . , When I was a baby . . . ,* and *When I was in kindergarten . . .* Post words such as *baby, teenager,* and *grandmother.* Include the *AlphaKids Guided Reader, My Baby Sister,* to remind children of the first stage of their life.

Book Browsing Center
Provide books about insects, such as *The Very Hungry Caterpillar* by Eric Carle and *Caterpillar Diary* by David Drew. Suggest that children read books about insects with a friend.

Birthday Cakes

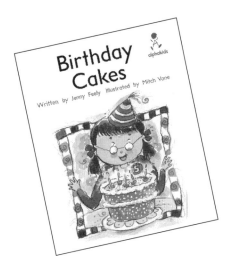

Text Features

- This book uses number words to explore a family's experience at birthday parties during the year.

- Repetitive text

- Two lines of text with a return sweep

- Uses the sentence forms ___ had ___ candles on his/her birthday cake. He/She blew them out with one big blow. The form changes near the end.

- Text supported by color illustrations

High-Frequency Words

had, on, her, his, He, She, with, them, we, said

Getting Ready for Reading

Discuss birthday parties children have been to. Focus on the ritual of the birthday cake. Ask: *What do the candles tell you? Who blows them out?*

Introducing the Book

You might say: *This is a book about birthdays a family celebrates during the year. Every time someone has a birthday, the family has a cake with the right number of candles on it. Then the candles are blown out with one big blow.* Turn to page 2 and say: *Here is Tina. How many candles are on her cake? Yes. She has two candles on her cake. She is two years old.* Turn to page 4 and say: *Lee is five. How many candles do you think Lee has on her cake?*

Reading the Book

As children read independently, listen to each child read small sections of the text and observe reading behaviors for ways to focus your guidance.

Selecting a Focus

Choose the role of the reader, from the *Kids As* menu, that meets the needs of this reading group. Later, you might return to this book to explore another reader's role.

CHECK THIS

Observe for evidence that children use all sources of information in the text. At the point of difficulty say: *Try that again and think of a word that would make sense. Does that word sound right? Does it look right?*

LITERACY CENTERS

Writing/Communication Center

Challenge children to help Grandma blow out her birthday candles. Have them complete a story starter, such as *I can help Grandma blow out the candles. I would . . .* Allow children to read their suggestions during Shared Reading.

ABC/Word Center

Display the words *blow* and *blew* on a sign entitled, *Words That Begin with /bl/.* Provide blue paper, magazines, glue, and scissors. Suggest that children write /bl/ on the paper; then cut out and glue pictures of /bl/ words to the paper.

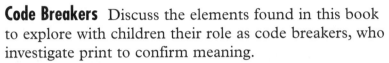

KIDS AS...

Meaning Makers Use questions like these to explore with children their role as meaning makers, who gather the book's basic message from print and pictures.

- *Which characters blew out the candles in one big blow?*
- *Did Grandma blow out the candles alone? Who helped? Is it easier to blow out candles when you are younger? Why?*

Code Breakers Discuss the elements found in this book to explore with children their role as code breakers, who investigate print to confirm meaning.

Vocabulary
Word families:
cake—make, lake, shake, take, bake, rake
had—Dad, sad, bad, lad, mad
blow—grow, flow, row, know, tow

Sounds and Letters
Hearing sounds:
/b/—birthday, big
/t/—Tina, ten, two
/bl/—blew, blow

Writing Conventions
Punctuation:
quotation marks
Grammar:
her/she and his/he

Text Users Use questions like these to help children explore how genre affects the information, the format, and the purpose of a book.

- *What order did the author use to show the birthdays? Would another order work?*
- *How do you know how old each family member is?*

Text Critics Use questions like these to explore how well the author and illustrator's work has met the book's purpose.

- *Do the family members look the same or different at each party? Does this makes sense? Why?*

LITERACY CENTERS

Interactive Literacy Center
Provide the story *The Three Little Pigs* in books or on cassette tape so that children might read or listen to the story with a friend. Encourage children to clap when they hear /bl/ words, especially *blow* and *blew*. Have pairs of children discuss what they would have done to the wolf if they were the pigs.

Book Browsing Center
Provide books about family traditions and encourage children to share and discuss books about family traditions. Have children illustrate their favorite family tradition. Encourage them to share their drawings with the class.

Tickling

Children might remember the characters in The Mailbox from *Guided Readers, Level 3.*

Text Features

- This book recounts the response of family members as they are tickled.
- Repetitive text
- One to five lines of text on a page
- Uses the sentence form *Anna tickled _____ on the _____.* And the response *"That's not funny," said _____.* The form changes near the end.
- Text supported by color illustrations

High-Frequency Words

a, on, the, that's, not, said, and, her

Getting Ready for Reading

Ask children: *Have you ever tickled someone? What did the person say? What did he or she do?* Talk about times children have tickled others or have been tickled. If possible, provide large feathers and let children explore how it feels to be tickled by a feather lightly touching their face.

Introducing the Book

You might say: *This book is about the time that Anna found a feather and tickled members of her family. They didn't think it was very funny.* Turn to page 4 and ask: *What did Anna do? Yes. She tickled Mom with a feather. What did Mom say? Yes, she said, "That's not funny."*

Reading the Book

As children read independently, listen to each child read small sections of the text and observe reading behaviors for ways to focus your guidance.

Selecting a Focus

Choose the role of the reader, from the *Kids As* menu, that meets the needs of this reading group. Later, you might return to this book to explore another reader's role.

CHECK THIS

Observe children's emergent reading behaviors for evidence of their ability to predict what would make sense. Prompt this by saying: *What would make sense in this sentence? Would* feather *fit? Does it look like* feather?

LITERACY CENTERS

Writing/Communication Center

Challenge children to think about what they would have done or said to Anna to show that her behavior was not funny. Have them write and illustrate a different ending to *Tickling.* Encourage children to share their endings with the class.

ABC/Word Center

Provide a chart entitled *Is It a Name?* Encourage children to read the room to find and list words that begin with a capital letter. Have them record the words on the chart. Challenge children to circle the words on the chart naming someone or something. Discuss the results when you meet.

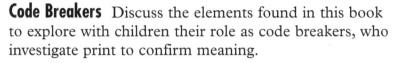

Meaning Makers Use questions like these to explore with children their role as meaning makers, who gather the book's basic message from print and pictures.

- *How did each character react to Anna's tickling?*
- *Did you guess what Mom was going to do with the feather on page 11? How could you tell?*

Code Breakers Discuss the elements found in this book to explore with children their role as code breakers, who investigate print to confirm meaning.

Vocabulary
Word families:
Dad—sad, bad, mad, had
not—dot, got, hot, lot, pot

Sounds and Letters
Hearing words:
Children clap for each word they hear in a sentence.
Hearing sounds:
/f/—foot, funny, feather

Writing Conventions
Punctuation:
periods, quotation marks, commas, and capital letters to begin names
Grammar:
word endings—tickled, tickling
contractions—that's/ that is

Text Users Use questions like these to help children explore how genre affects the information, the format, and the purpose of a book.

- *How do the pictures help you know what the words say?*

Text Critics Use questions like these to explore how well the author and illustrator's work has met the book's purpose.

- *How does the illustrator show how the family members feel when tickled? Do you like this way? Why?*
- *How might another family act when tickled?*

LITERACY CENTERS

Book Browsing Center
Invite children to choose a book from the Book Browsing Center that has a word beginning with *f* in its title. Have pairs of children read their selections to each other. Ask children to listen for words in the story that begin with *f*.

Interactive Literacy Center
Invite children to retell *Tickling* to a friend. If they created a new ending at the *Writing/Communication Center*, encourage them to use their ending as they retell the story. Encourage children to use expression as they retell the story.

Rain

Text Features

- This book is about a child's attempts to dress appropriately during one week of rain.
- Repetitive, cumulative text
- One to seven lines of text on a page
- Uses the sentence forms *It rained on ___. I put on my ___ and my ___. I went outside. My ___ got wet.*
- Text supported by color illustrations
- Text clearly separated from illustrations

High-Frequency Words

It, on, I, put, my, and, went, came, go

Getting Ready for Reading

Talk about clothing we wear to go outside in the rain. Ask: *What might you wear on your feet? head?* Have children help you make a chart by telling you about clothing they might wear in the rain. Ask children to explain what might happen if they didn't wear each item. Record children's responses on the chart.

Introducing the Book

Introduce the book by saying: *This book is about a boy who didn't wear the clothes that would keep him dry in the rain.* You might discuss the boy's decisions: *The boy went outside on Monday. It rained. His whole body got wet. What did he do on Tuesday? Yes, he put on his raincoat and went outside again.* Ask: *Do you think he stayed dry this time? What else might he need to wear?*

Reading the Book

As children read independently, listen to each child read small sections of the text and observe reading behaviors for ways to focus your guidance.

Selecting a Focus

Choose the role of the reader, from the *Kids As* menu, that meets the needs of this reading group. Later, you might return to this book to explore another reader's role.

CHECK THIS

Observe for evidence that children use punctuation to support fluent reading. Remind them to pause at commas and periods.

LITERACY CENTERS

Writing/Communication Center

Provide photos or drawings of types of weather. Include the weather words, such as *rain, snow, hail, tornado,* and *sun.* Randomly display pictures and weather words in the center. Invite children to match each weather word to the picture it describes.

ABC/Word Center

Provide a set of 8 word cards that say *-et* and a set of cards containing the consonants *w, g, b, s, m, n, l, p.* Have children join the consonant cards to the *-et* cards to form words in the *-et* word family. Then suggest that children read each word to a friend.

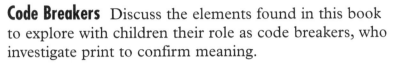

KIDS AS...

Meaning Makers Use questions like these to explore with children their role as meaning makers, who gather the book's basic message from print and pictures.

- *What did the boy learn on Monday? What did he do then?*
- *How many days did the boy go outside?*
  Why do you think the boy didn't go outside on Sunday?

Code Breakers Discuss the elements found in this book to explore with children their role as code breakers, who investigate print to confirm meaning.

Vocabulary
Word families:
wet—get, bet, set, met, net, let, pet
went—bent, cent, dent, sent, tent
it—bit, fit, hit, lit, pit, sit

Writing Conventions
Punctuation:
capital letters, periods, and commas
Grammar:
contractions—didn't/ did not

Sounds and Letters
Hearing sounds:
short /e/—went, wet

Text Users Use questions like these to help children explore how genre affects the information, the format, and the purpose of a book.

- *What does this book tell you about the boy? about the rain?*
- *Why do you think the author had the boy put on one item of clothing at a time instead of putting them on all at once?*

Text Critics Use questions like these to explore how well the author and illustrator's work has met the book's purpose.

- *Did you like the book's illustrations? Why?*
- *What would you tell a friend about this book?*

rain   snow
sun   hail

LITERACY CENTERS

Interactive Literacy Center
Have pairs of children illustrate their favorite type of weather. Then invite one child to hold up the illustration, while the other child acts as a meteorologist, reporting on the weather conditions in the picture. Suggest that partners reverse roles, giving each child an opportunity to be a meteorologist.

Book Browsing Center
Provide books about weather, the AlphaKids Alphabet Books for R and S, books about playing outside, and books about the days of the week. Have children choose their favorite book to read to a friend.

Twins

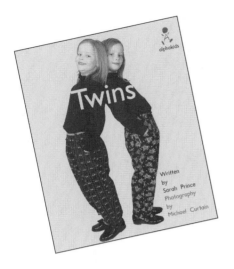

Text Features

- This book is about identical twins.
- Some repetitive text
- Two to three lines of text
- Uses the sentence forms *We have the same ____. Look at our ____.* and *We ___ different things. I like ___. She likes ____.*
- Text supported by color photos
- Text clearly separated from photos

High-Frequency Words

my, and, I, are, we, look, have, the, same, at, our, do, like, eat, she

Getting Ready for Reading

Play *Same and Different*. Have children work in pairs to choose two items in the classroom, then identify things about the items that are the same and different. As children share, model the form of the text as closely as possible. You might say: *Chalk and paper are the same color. They are both white. They do different things. Chalk is for writing with and paper is for writing on.* Then discuss the concept of twins. If you have twins in your class, ask them to talk about what it is like to be a twin.

Introducing the Book

Talk through the book by saying: *This is a book about twins. It shows us how the twins are the same and how they are different.* Turn to page 4 and say: *For the first half of the book, the twins tell us how they are the same.* Turn to page 10 and say: *Then the twins tell us how they are different.*

Reading the Book

As children read independently, listen to each child read small sections of the text and observe reading behaviors for ways to focus your guidance.

Selecting a Focus

Choose the role of the reader, from the *Kids As* menu, that meets the needs of this reading group. Later, you might return to this book to explore another reader's role.

CHECK THIS

Observe for evidence that children know that good readers self-check as they read. Prompts to promote this might be: *How did you know that word was right? What did you do to work that word out by yourself?*

LITERACY CENTERS

Writing/Communication Center

Have pairs of children each choose an animal and write ways their animal is the same as their partner's and ways it is different. Their papers might read: *A moose and a bear both have fur. They like to eat different things. A moose likes grass. A bear likes fish.*

ABC/Word Center

Provide small squares of paper and crayons. Direct children to draw an item on one square and two or more of the same item on another square. Have groups of children pool their squares to play *Memory*, matching the single images on the squares to the plurals.

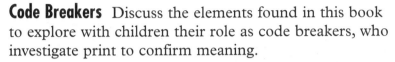

KIDS AS...

Meaning Makers Use questions like these to explore with children their role as meaning makers, who gather the book's basic message from print and pictures.

- *How are the twins the same? How are the twins different?*
- *How might you tell one twin from the other?*

Code Breakers Discuss the elements found in this book to explore with children their role as code breakers, who investigate print to confirm meaning.

Vocabulary
Word families:
same—blame, came, flame, game, name, tame

Sounds and Letters
Hearing sounds:
/s/—sister, same, soccer

Writing Conventions
Punctuation:
capital letters and periods
Grammar:
plural nouns—twins, eyes, bananas, apples

Text Users Use questions like these to help children explore how genre affects the information, the format, and the purpose of a book.

- *Is this book fictional or factual? How do you know?*
- *How is the first part of the book different from the second? Could the author tell us about the twins in a different way? How?*

Text Critics Use questions like these to explore how well the author and photographer's work has met the book's purpose.

- *What is the author trying to tell us about twins? Do you think this is true?*
- *Do the photos help you understand what the author is saying? Would drawings work better, the same, or not as well?*

> A moose and a bear both have fur. They like to eat different things.

LITERACY CENTERS

Interactive Literacy Center
Have groups of three children role-play interviews. Two children play the twins and the third child is the interviewer. Encourage the children to switch roles to allow each child a turn as the interviewer. Remind the children that, when the answer to an interview question is not given in the book, they should be creative and make one up.

Book Browsing Center
Encourage children to browse books for people or animals they think look the same. Some people in the books all might have yellow hair. Some animals all might have long necks. Have children show their books to a friend and share what they think looks the same.

What's That Noise?

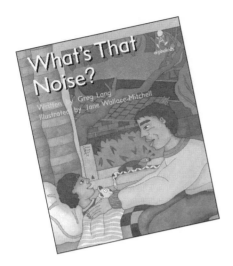

Text Features

- This book is about a boy who tries to stay up by asking about the noises he hears at bedtime.

- Onomatopoeia is introduced.

- Three lines of text on each page except the last

- Uses the sentence forms *"What's that noise?" asked Hector. "That's a/the _____ the _____," said Dad.* The sentence form changes on the last two pages.

- Text supported by color illustrations

High-Frequency Words

What's, that, That's, a, on, the, said, down, in, up, me, off, asked

Getting Ready for Reading

Talk about children who try to stay awake at bedtime. Ask: *What are some things children might do to stay up longer? What might their parents say and do?*

Introducing the Book

Talk through the book by saying: *This is a book about a boy named Hector who tries to stay up at bedtime. He does it by asking his dad about the noises he hears from his bedroom.* Turn to pages 2 and 3. You might point to the sound word in the illustration and say: *What sound do you think is coming in the window? Let's say it together. What do you think is making the sound. Yes, a police siren could be making the sound.*

Reading the Book

As children read independently, listen to each child read small sections of the text and observe reading behaviors for ways to focus your guidance.

Selecting a Focus

Choose the role of the reader, from the *Kids As* menu, that meets the needs of this reading group. Later, you might return to this book to explore another reader's role.

CHECK THIS

Observe for evidence that children self-correct while reading the text. Comment positively on self-correcting behavior. You might say: *Well done. You corrected yourself. You chose a word that makes sense.*

LITERACY CENTERS

Writing/Communication Center
Provide construction paper and crayons or markers. Challenge children to write a word that describes a sound they might hear in the classroom or at home. Then have them illustrate that sound. Encourage them to show the onomatopoeia in their illustration.

ABC/Word Center
Write high-frequency and –at and –ar words on cards. Randomly display the cards in a pocket chart. Provide a blank stack of cards for writing more words. Invite children to work together to form sentences and then read them aloud.

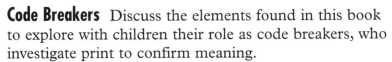

KIDS AS...

Meaning Makers Use questions like these to explore with children their role as meaning makers, who gather the book's basic message from print and pictures.

- *What noises does Hector hear? Does Hector know what is making the noises? Why do you think he keeps asking?*
- *Why do you think the baby wakes up?*

Code Breakers Discuss the elements found in this book to explore with children their role as code breakers, who investigate print to confirm meaning.

Vocabulary
Word families:
that—bat, cat, fat, hat, mat, rat, sat
car—far, jar, star

Sounds and Letters
Hearing sounds:
/at/ in what and that

Writing Conventions
Punctuation:
question marks, quotation marks, and commas
Grammar:
dialogue words—asked/said
Onomatopoeia:
ee-ow, brmm, woof, meeow, wah, click

Text Users Use questions like these to help children explore how genre affects the information, the format, and the purpose of a book.

- *What do the sound words in the pictures tell you?*
- *Which part of the book would you call the ending? What other endings can you think of for this story?*

Text Critics Use questions like these to explore how well the author and illustrator's work has met the book's purpose.

- *What is the author saying about how children feel about bedtime?*
- *Would you recommend this book? Why?*
- *Do the sound words make the story better? Why?*

LITERACY CENTERS

Interactive Literacy Center
Have pairs of children read *What's That Noise?* and record the story on cassette tape. Suggest that they close their eyes and listen to their tape after recording it. Later, you might discuss how hearing the story was different from reading it.

Book Browsing Center
Invite children to search for stories about times they might wish to avoid, such as eating broccoli or visiting a doctor. Suggest that they read their book to a friend and discuss creative ways they might find to make these times more fun.

Making Butter

Text Features

- This book recounts the process involved in making butter at school.
- Nonrepetitive text
- One to five lines of text on a page
- Sentence form and length vary; a list of ingredients is introduced.
- Text supported by color illustrations

High-Frequency Words

We, at, a, of, some, with, put, in, the, looked, there, but, was, no, and, into, all, It

Getting Ready for Reading

Make butter with your groups. Provide a jar with a screw top, about a cup of cream for each group, some salt, and a strainer. While children shake the jar, model the form of the text, using words such as buttermilk and strainer. Eat and enjoy!

Introducing the Book

You might introduce the book by saying: *This is a book about children making butter at school.* Focus on the list on page 4, and compare the quantities with those your group used. On each page ask: *What can you see happening here?* Respond by modeling the text. For example, on pages 6 and 7, you might say: *The children put the cream and the salt in the jar. They put the lid on the jar.*

Reading the Book

As children read independently, listen to each child read small sections of the text and observe reading behaviors for ways to focus your guidance.

Selecting a Focus

Choose the role of the reader, from the *Kids As* menu, that meets the needs of this reading group. Later, you might return to this book to explore another reader's role.

CHECK THIS

Observe for evidence that children recognize and pay attention to print information. You might point to the initial letter or clusters of letters and ask: *Do you know a word that begins with the same letter or letters that this word begins with?*

LITERACY CENTERS

Writing/Communication Center

Display menus listing pizza toppings. Provide white construction paper and crayons. Challenge children to draw a pizza with their favorite toppings. Have them write a list of the toppings they chose. Encourage pairs of children to compare their lists.

ABC/Word Center

Provide words cards for: *need, talk, make, jump, shake, run, tip, needed, talked, made, jumped, shook, ran, tipped.* Have pairs of children make up a game in which they match each word in the past tense to its form in the present tense.

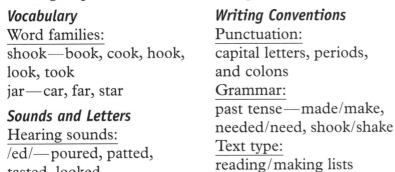

KIDS AS...

Meaning Makers Use questions like these to explore with children their role as meaning makers, who gather the book's basic message from print and pictures.

- *What did the children use to make butter? After shaking the jar, what was in it?*
- *How long did it take to make butter? How do you know?*

Code Breakers Discuss the elements found in this book to explore with children their role as code breakers, who investigate print to confirm meaning.

Vocabulary
Word families:
shook—book, cook, hook, look, took
jar—car, far, star

Sounds and Letters
Hearing sounds:
/ed/—poured, patted, tasted, looked

Writing Conventions
Punctuation:
capital letters, periods, and colons
Grammar:
past tense—made/make, needed/need, shook/shake
Text type:
reading/making lists

Text Users Use questions like these to help children explore how genre affects the information, the format, and the purpose of a book.

- *Would you use this book to make butter? Why?*
- *Would this book make sense if the events were in a different order? Why?*

Text Critics Use questions like these to explore how well the author and illustrator's work has met the book's purpose.

- *Why might a clock appear in some pictures? Do you think this was a good idea? Why?*

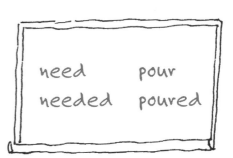

need   pour
needed   poured

LITERACY CENTERS

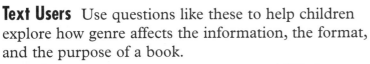

Interactive Literacy Center
Have pairs of children teach each other how to make butter. Encourage them to act out the steps given in the book. Then invite children to teach each other another process. Offer suggestions such as tying shoelaces, making a peanut butter and jelly sandwich, folding a paper airplane, setting a table, or building a snowman or a sand castle.

Book Browsing Center
Provide books about food, such as *Pancakes For Breakfast* by Tomie dePaola and *Green Eggs and Ham* by Dr. Seuss. Have pairs of children choose a book to read together and discuss how they might go about making the food in the story.

I Can't Find My Roller Skates

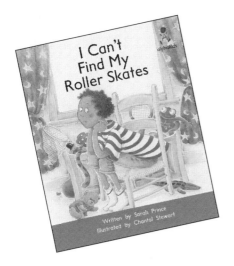

Getting Ready for Reading

Talk about times when things have been lost in the classroom. Ask: *Where did we need to look?* Emphasize positional words, such as *in, on, up, under,* and *behind.*

Introducing the Book

Talk through the book by saying: *This is a book about lost roller skates. The girl who has lost them looks everywhere.* Turn through the book, noting with children the places she looks. *She looked in the toy box. They weren't in there. She looked on the bookshelf, upstairs, under the bed, and behind the door. She looked everywhere.*

Reading the Book

As children read independently, listen to each child read small sections of the text and observe reading behaviors for ways to focus your guidance.

Selecting a Focus

Choose the role of the reader, from the *Kids As* menu, that meets the needs of this reading group. Later, you might return to this book to explore another reader's role.

Text Features

- This book is about a girl's efforts to find her roller skates.
- Repetitive text
- One line of text per page with sentence crossing to next page
- Uses the sentence form *I looked ____ the ____, but they weren't ____ there.*
- Text supported by color illustrations

High-Frequency Words

I, can't, my, lost, the, but, they, there, on, for, in, up

CHECK THIS

Observe for evidence that children use cues from all sources. Some prompts to promote this might be: *What word might you try? What word would make sense? Can you think of a word that sounds right?*

LITERACY CENTERS

Writing/Communication Center
Suggest the story starter *Once I lost ____.* Have children write a story that includes what they lost, if they found it, and how they found it.

ABC/Word Center
Provide two sets of word cards—one set showing contractions and another set showing the words each contraction is made up of. Have children match each contraction to its full form. Then invite children to play school by teaching a friend how contractions work.

KIDS AS...

Meaning Makers Use questions like these to explore with children their role as meaning makers, who gather the book's basic message from print and pictures.

- ◆ *How did the girl find the roller skates?*
- ◆ *Does the girl's sister know the girl wanted the skates?*

Code Breakers Discuss the elements found in this book to explore with children their role as code breakers, who investigate print to confirm meaning.

Vocabulary
Word families:
skate—ate, date, fate, gate, hate, late, rate
think—blink, ink, link, pink, rink, sink, wink
but—cut, gut, hut, jut, nut
Positional words:
in, on, up, under, behind

Sounds and Letters
Hearing sounds:
/oo/—looked, book

Writing Conventions
Punctuation:
exclamation marks, commas, and apostrophes
Grammar:
contractions—can't/cannot, weren't/were not, haven't/have not

Text Users Use questions like these to help children explore how genre affects the information, the format, and the purpose of a book.

- ◆ *How do you know where the girl looks for her roller skates?*
- ◆ *Where could we see the girl's sister? Why?*

Text Critics Use questions like these to explore how well the author and illustrator's work has met the book's purpose.

- ◆ *Do problems like this happen in most families? Why do you think so?*
- ◆ *Was this story fun to read? Why?*

Once I lost . . .

LITERACY CENTERS

Interactive Literacy Center
Invite pairs of children to play *Guess My Object*. Have one child first select an object in the classroom that is visible from the center and provide the other child with clues, such as *It is on the bookshelf and has a blue cover.* Have the other child try to guess what the object might be.

Book Browsing Center
Challenge children to search text in such resources as storybooks, information books, magazines, or posters to find and list as many positional words as they can. Have them read the words with a friend.

Making Lunch

Children might remember Uncle Vin, Anna, and Sam from earlier *AlphaKids Guided Readers.*

Text Features

- This book is about two children who are too busy to help their uncle.

- Repetitive text

- Two to nine lines of text per page

- Uses the sentence forms: *"I'm making _____," said Uncle Vin."* Who will help me? *"Not me," said ___. "I'm too busy."* The form changes toward the end.

- Text supported by color illustrations

High-Frequency Words

I'm, said, You, me, too, will, Not, can, and, were, make, to, Who

Getting Ready for Reading

You might ask: *Have you ever told someone you were too busy to do something he or she asked you to do? What did he or she say? What did he or she do? Were you always too busy or did you sometimes just want to avoid doing what you were asked to do?* Explore the form of the text by saying: *I'm washing the dishes* (or other household chore). *Who will help me?* Children might respond by saying: *Not me, I'm too busy.*

Introducing the Book

You might introduce the book by saying:
> *In this book Uncle Vin has trouble getting Sam and Anna to help him make lunch. He tries to get them to help him make soup, sandwiches, orange juice, and fruit salad, but they are always too busy.*

Reading the Book

As children read independently, listen to each child read small sections of the text and observe reading behaviors for ways to focus your guidance.

Selecting a Focus

Choose the role of the reader, from the *Kids As* menu, that meets the needs of this reading group. Later, you might return to this book to explore another reader's role.

CHECK THIS

Observe for evidence that children self-correct their errors while reading. A prompt to promote this is: *That was almost right. Can you find the part that was hard for you? How might you use a word like this one to help you figure this other one out?*

LITERACY CENTERS

Writing/Communication Center
Have children write Sam and Anna a letter of advice on how to be more helpful and kind. You might display a sample letter for reference, reviewing the letter's components. Allow children to read their letter to a friend.

ABC/Word Center
Provide magazines and have children cut out a magazine picture in which people are talking. Suggest that children tell a friend a story about the conversation in the picture that uses the words *asked* or *said.*

KIDS AS...

Meaning Makers Use questions like these to explore with children their role as meaning makers, who gather the book's basic message from print and pictures.

◆ *How do you know the children were too busy to help?*

◆ *What lesson was Uncle Vin teaching Sam and Anna? Did they learn it? Why do you think so?*

Code Breakers Discuss the elements found in this book to explore with children their role as code breakers, who investigate print to confirm meaning.

Vocabulary
Word families:
not—hot, cot, rot, dot, plot, got, pot, spot
Homophones:
too/to/two

Sounds and Letters
Hearing words:
Children clap for each word in a sentence.

    ★ ★ ★
   I'm too busy.

Hearing sounds:
/oo/—who, too, you

Writing Conventions
Punctuation:
quotation marks, commas, question marks, periods, and capital letters to begin names
Grammar:
contractions—I'm/I am
direct speech

Text Users Use questions like these to help children explore how genre affects the information, the format, and the purpose of a book.

◆ *How do you know who says, "Who will help me?"*

◆ *Why does Uncle Vin list the chores Sam and Anna don't do? How else might people use a list?*

Text Critics Use questions like these to explore how well the author and illustrator's work has met the book's purpose.

◆ *Is the author's message about helping others clear?*

◆ *Do the illustrations on pages 13 and 15 show how Sam and Anna feel?*

LITERACY CENTERS

Interactive Literacy Center
Challenge groups of three children to be the characters Anna, Sam, and Uncle Vin. Have children read the text aloud. Then have children role-play the story as an interactive retelling.

Book Browsing Center
Have children find a book with dialogue and read it with a partner. Suggest that partners look through the book after reading to find examples of quotation marks.

Looking for Fang

Children might remember Uncle Vin, Dad, Anna, and Sam from earlier AlphaKids Guided Readers.

Text Features

- This book recounts the efforts of a girl and her community to find her pet.
- Repetitive text
- Cumulative text
- Uses the sentence form: *"We're looking for Fang," said ____.* and the response *"What does he look like?" asked ____.*
- Text supported by color illustrations
- Text placed consistently on the page

High-Frequency Words

said, I'm, for, he, has, Have, you, him, and, a, here

Getting Ready for Reading

Play *Have you seen it?* Select an object from the classroom. Tell children that you will call the mystery object a "dreedle." Say: *I'm looking for a dreedle. Have you seen it?* Explain that children might say: *No, what does it look like?* in response. Give children clues until they identify the object.

Introducing the Book

You might say: *This is a book about something that is lost. Jo has lost Fang and is looking for him. What do you think Fang could be? Jo sees her next-door neighbor and asks for help looking.* Page through the book, except for the last page. Say: *By the end of the book we know that Fang has great big ears, sharp claws, big white teeth, gray hair, and a short tail.* Ask children to predict what Fang might be.

Reading the Book

As children read independently, listen to each child read small sections of the text and observe reading behaviors for ways to focus your guidance.

Selecting a Focus

Choose the role of the reader, from the *Kids As* menu, that meets the needs of this reading group. Later, you might return to this book to explore another reader's role.

CHECK THIS

Observe for evidence that children self-check their reading. After an error occurs, prompts to promote this could be: *Check what you read. Does the word sound right? Does it look right? It could be __ but look at the first letter.*

LITERACY CENTERS

Writing/Communication Center

Provide butcher paper or poster board, markers, samples of addresses, and decorative materials. Have children create a "missing poster" for Fang that includes a picture, a description, Jo's name and pretend address, and a reward for finding Fang.

ABC/Word Center

Display *look, book, cook, hook, dig, wig, pig,* and *big*. Provide oaktag squares. Have pairs of children take eight squares; one child writes -ook words on four squares, while the other writes -ig words on four. Have partners pool their cards and take turns selecting a card. Challenge them to make up a sentence using the two word cards they have selected.

KIDS AS...

Meaning Makers Use questions like these to explore with children their role as meaning makers, who gather the book's basic message from print and pictures.
- *Did you know what kind of animal Fang was? How?*
- *Why is Jo looking for Fang? Who helped Jo look?*

Code Breakers Discuss the elements found in this book to explore with children their role as code breakers, who investigate print to confirm meaning.

Vocabulary
Word families:
look—book, took, shook, cook, hook
big—dig, fig, pig, wig

Sounds and Letters
Hearing sounds:
/h/—here, has, have, help, hair, he, him

Writing Conventions
Punctuation:
quotation marks, question marks, commas, and apostrophes
Grammar:
building words—look/looking
question words—What's, Have
contractions—we're, I'm, I'll

Text Users Use questions like these to help children explore how genre affects the information, the format, and the purpose of a book.
- *What could you learn from reading this book?*
- *Why does Jo repeat her description of Fang so many times?*

Text Critics Use questions like these to explore how well the author and illustrator's work has met the book's purpose.
- *Why did Jo only describe Fang? Did it make the book more interesting? Why?*
- *Should Fang's name have described him better? Why?*

LITERACY CENTERS

Interactive Literacy Center
Place small objects from the classroom, that children are somewhat familiar with, in a bag. Invite children to play *Have you seen it?* with a friend. Have one child put an object from the bag behind his or her back. He or she might give clues, such as: "It has numbers and lots of buttons. Have you seen it?" The response might be: "It's a calculator. It's behind your back."

Book Browsing Center
Have children browse encyclopedias and storybooks to find animals that they might keep as a pet. Encourage them to share the book with a friend and to tell their friend what they would name the animal.

Tadpoles and Frogs

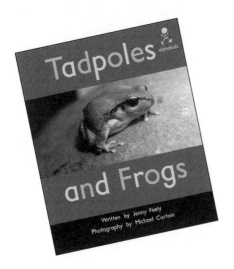

Written by Jenny Feely
Photography by Michael Curtain

Text Features

- This is a factual text about the life cycle of a frog.
- Nonrepetitive text
- Two or three lines of text on a page
- Uses a diagram
- Text supported by color photos
- Text placed consistently on the page

High-Frequency Words

The, on, from, and, in, is, a

Getting Ready for Reading

Explore together a children's encyclopedia article about the life cycle of a frog. Discuss the changes that take place as the frog grows from a tadpole. Invite children who have seen frogs or tadpoles to share their experiences.

Introducing the Book

Introduce the book by saying: *This book explains the stages a frog's egg goes through as it grows up to be a frog.* Talk through the book, asking: *What has happened now?* Say: *Yes, the frog has laid eggs on the water. Tadpoles have hatched from the eggs. The tadpole's back legs have grown. Look at the photograph. Can you see how the tadpole is changing?*

Reading the Book

As children read independently, listen to each child read small sections of the text and observe reading behaviors for ways to focus your guidance.

Selecting a Focus

Choose the role of the reader, from the *Kids As* menu, that meets the needs of this reading group. Later, you might return to this book to explore another reader's role.

CHECK THIS

Observe for evidence that children use visual information when reading the text. Prompts to promote this might be: *Look at the end of the word. What word do you know that ends like that? What word might you try?*

LITERACY CENTERS

Writing/Communication Center
Randomly display sentences from the text written on sentence strips. Place them in a pocket chart. Have children sequence the sentences according to the text, then illustrate what might happen after the tadpole becomes a frog. Discuss their illustrations together.

ABC/Word Center
Have children browse books to find words in the text that begin with the sound /fr/. Ask them to use letter cards to make a collage or puzzle from the /fr/ words they found. Challenge them to include any other words they know that begin with this sound.

KIDS AS...

Meaning Makers Use questions like these to explore with children their role as meaning makers, who gather the book's basic message from print and pictures.

◆ *Can you describe the changes that happen to the tadpole as it grows?*

◆ *What might happen next in the frog's life?*

Code Breakers Discuss the elements found in this book to explore with children their role as code breakers, who investigate print to confirm meaning.

Vocabulary
Word families:
and—band, hand, land, sand

Sounds and Letters
Hearing sounds:
/fr/—from, frog, front

Writing Conventions
Punctuation:
periods and possessive apostrophes—tadpole's
Grammar:
possessive form—tadpole's
Text types:
diagrams

Text Users Use questions like these to help children explore how genre affects the information, the format, and the purpose of a book.

◆ *Why does this book use photographs instead of illustrations? How is this book different from a storybook?*

◆ *What does the diagram on the last page show?*

Text Critics Use questions like these to explore how well the author and photographer's work has met the book's purpose.

◆ *Which part of this book presents information best— diagrams, photographs, or sentences?*

◆ *What information might be added to better understand the frog's life?*

LITERACY CENTERS

Book Browsing Center
Encourage pairs of children to browse encyclopedias to find animals that are smaller than a frog. Provide copies of *Ranger Rick* and *National Geographic*, if available, for further reference. Later, invite children to share what they found.

Interactive Literacy Center
Have pairs of children make up and perform a commercial selling pet frogs and tadpoles. Suggest that they use what they've learned about frogs to make their commercial more interesting.

Going Shopping

Text Features

- This book uses alliteration to explore the items for sale at many types of stores.
- Repetitive text
- One to four lines of text on a page. Text appears on color background.
- Uses the sentence forms *I'm going shopping at the _____. What will I buy— _____? No. _____!*
- Text supported by color illustrations

High-Frequency Words

I'm, going, at, the, What, will, I, no

Getting Ready for Reading

Provide each child with a label naming a store from the text, such as *bakery, pet store, florist, hardware store, toy store,* and *supermarket.* Ask children to tell you three things that they could buy at the store on their label.

Introducing the Book

You might say: *This is a book about different stores and the things you might buy there.* Walk through the book by asking: *If I'm going shopping at the bakery, will I buy beans, buttons, babies, or books?* Have children model the text and respond with *No. Bread!* Point out the labels within the illustrations that match the objects in the text.

Reading the Book

As children read independently, listen to each child read small sections of the text and observe reading behaviors for ways to focus your guidance.

Selecting a Focus

Choose the role of the reader, from the *Kids As* menu, that meets the needs of this reading group. Later, you might return to this book to explore another reader's role.

CHECK THIS

Observe children's emergent reading behaviors for evidence that their reading is phrased and fluent. Prompts to promote this are: *Remember to read words like a question. Put your words together to make them sound like talking.*

LITERACY CENTERS

Writing/Communication Center
Have children choose one store from the story to complete the sentence forms *I'm going shopping at _____. I will buy _____ and _____.* Suggest that they illustrate their purchases.

ABC/Word Center
Provide catalogs and scissors. Invite children to cut out pictures of things that begin with /sh/. Have them tape the pictures to a mural entitled *Things That Begin with /sh/.*

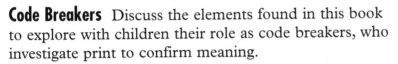

KIDS AS...

Meaning Makers Use questions like these to explore with children their role as meaning makers, who gather the book's basic message from print and pictures.

◆ *Why does the boy say, "What will I buy?"*
◆ *What kind of tigers can you buy at a toy store? Are those kinds of tigers included in this story?*

Code Breakers Discuss the elements found in this book to explore with children their role as code breakers, who investigate print to confirm meaning.

Vocabulary
Word lists for alliteration:
books, buttons, babies, beans, boots, bats, bread

Sounds and Letters
Hearing sounds:
/b/, /p/, /f/, /h/, /s/, /t/
Hearing blends and digraphs:
/fl/, /tr/, /sh/

Writing Conventions
Punctuation:
capital letters, periods, question marks, dashes, and exclamation marks
Text types:
labels

Text Users Use questions like these to help children explore how genre affects the information, the format, and the purpose of a book.

◆ *What would this book help you find out about stores?*
◆ *What do you notice about the items named in each store? Why did the author choose those items?*

Text Critics Use questions like these to explore how well the author and illustrator's work has met the book's purpose.

◆ *Why were labels included in the art? Was it a good idea?*
◆ *Did you think the ending of the book makes sense? How might you change the ending?*

LITERACY CENTERS

Interactive Literacy Center
Challenge groups of three to chant *I'm going to the market.* Invite one child to begin by chanting *I'm going to the market and I'm going to buy some _____.* Have the others repeat the items and add what they would buy. Encourage the group to recall what all three children said.

Book Browsing Center
Have children search a picture dictionary or magazine for other things that might be purchased at the stores mentioned in the story. Suggest they also look for items that are found in the store they wrote about in the *Writing/Communication Center*.

Plants

Text Features

- This book is about the things all plants need to live.
- Repetitive text
- Sentence length varies.
- Uses several sentence forms.
- Text supported by color photos and illustrations
- Text appears in diagrams.

High-Frequency Words

All, and, from, get, the, a, is, It, There, are, of, they

Getting Ready for Reading

Discuss the needs of plants. Talk about what happens to plants when they do not get water or sunlight. Have children pretend to be plants by turning their hands up, like leaves, toward the sun. You might have children suck water from a cup with straws to illustrate plants sucking water through their roots. Use the language of the book as you guide children in these activities.

Introducing the Book

You might say: *This is a book that gives information about plants.* Turn to page 2 and talk through the layout of the page. Say: *This page tells us that all plants need food and water. It says that a plant's leaves make food from sunlight and its roots get water from the ground.* Explain the use of labels and pointer lines in the diagram on page 9.

Reading the Book

As children read independently, listen to each child read small sections of the text and observe reading behaviors for ways to focus your guidance.

Selecting a Focus

Choose the role of the reader, from the *Kids As* menu, that meets the needs of this reading group. Later, you might return to this book to explore another reader's role.

CHECK THIS

Observe children's emergent reading behaviors for evidence of problem solving when reading text. A prompt to promote this might be: *Try reading that sentence again and think what word would make sense and sound right.*

LITERACY CENTERS

Writing/Communication Center
Challenge children to illustrate an imaginary plant that would never need water. Have children label the plant's parts and draw the environment in which the plant lives. Invite them to show and tell the class why their plant does not need water.

ABC/Word Center
Provide a poem or short text about plants, sentence strips, counters, and markers. Have children copy a sentence from the poem or text onto a sentence strip. Then challenge them to place counters on the syllables of each word to show how many syllables the word has.

KIDS AS...

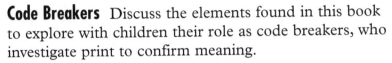

Meaning Makers Use questions like these to explore with children their role as meaning makers, who gather the book's basic message from print and pictures.

- *What do plants need to live? Do all plants need these things? How do you know?*
- *What do sun and rain give plants?*

Code Breakers Discuss the elements found in this book to explore with children their role as code breakers, who investigate print to confirm meaning.

Vocabulary
Word families:
all—ball, call, fall, hall, mall, tall, wall
and—band, hand, land, sand

Writing Conventions
Punctuation:
capital letters and periods
Text types:
diagrams

Sounds and Letters
Hearing words:
Children place counters for each syllable they hear.

★ ★   ★   ★   ★
wa‑ter   ground   sun‑light

Text Users Use questions like these to help children explore how genre affects the information, the format, and the purpose of a book.

- *What does this book teach you? What does page 16 tell you?*

Text Critics Use questions like these to explore the success of the author's, illustrator's, and photographer's work.

- *What did the author need to know to write this book? How could you find out if she gave good information?*

LITERACY CENTERS

Interactive Literacy Center
Display a plant you have created for children to refer to. Provide pipe cleaners, tissue paper in many colors, glue, and butcher paper. Encourage pairs of children to create a flowering plant with the materials, and glue it to the butcher paper. Have them diagram, around the plant, what their plant might need to survive. Allow children to tell the class about their plant.

Book Browsing Center
Invite children to find books in the Book Browsing Center about plants. You also might include gardening books or seed packets for children to read. Suggest that children observe which books have an index page.

Records of Reading Behaviors

Records of Reading Behaviors are based on the Running Records that are work of Marie Clay (1993). The main difference between the two assessments is that while a running record is taken "on the run," making notations on blank paper, a record of reading behaviors is taken using a transcript of the text and keeps the text tied to the record of performance. Both procedures offer the teacher valuable information about a child's current reading behaviors. The running record requires less preparation, since no text transcript is needed. The record of reading behaviors, however, provides a lasting report of performance for later analysis and for conferencing with parents.

Since both assessments are used with texts the child has not yet read, you might wish to save one book at each level for this purpose. On the pages that follow are already prepared transcripts from five of the AlphaKids Guided Readers. These reproducible pages provide the text of one book representative of each level of difficulty. A blank form is also provided to allow you to include additional texts as benchmark books for taking a record of reading behaviors at each level.

Taking a Record of Reading Behaviors

correct	tick the word	✔ ✔ ✔ ✔ ✔ Can you see my eyes?
miscue	write the spoken word above the word in the text	✔ ✔✔ the ✔ Can you see my eyes?
insertion	insert the spoken word using a ^	✔ ✔ ✔ ✔ big ✔ Can you see my ^eyes?
omission	place a line above the word left out	✔ ✔ ✔ __ ✔ Can you see my eyes?
repetition	write R after the repeated word(s)	✔ ✔ ✔✔ R ✔ Can you see my eyes?
attempt	write the word attempted above the word	✔ ✔ ✔ ✔ e ey Can you see my eyes?
asks for help	write A above the appeal	✔ ✔ ✔ A ✔ Can you see my eyes?
told word	write T above the word	✔ ✔ ✔ T ✔ Can you see my eyes?
no response	place a line above the word	✔ ✔ ✔ _ ✔ Can you see my eyes?
self-corrects	write SC after the miscue	✔ ✔ ✔ the I SC ✔ Can you see my eyes?

With early readers, a monthly record of reading behaviors is taken by:

1. selecting a book at the child's instructional level that the child has not yet read.

2. asking the child to read the new book orally.

3. marking carefully on a transcript of the same text the child's correct responses and miscues as he or she reads the text.

Researchers and practitioners[1] have formalized a system of notations that make recording a child's performance as efficient, clear, and nonintrusive as possible.

[1] Based on Clay 1993, Kemp 1987, Godman & Burke 1972.

Scoring a Reader's Performance

You can use the following scoring to evaluate a child's performance, as taken by a record of reading behaviors.

1. Count only running words in a text. Running words do not include titles and subtitles, and so on.

2. Count as 1 error:
   - miscues
   - omissions
   - insertions
   - told words (words supplied for the reader)
   - no response
   - each word in a skipped line

3. Count a skipped page as 1 error and subtract the word count for that page from the total word count.

4. Count proper nouns read inaccurately only once. Count other words read inaccurately each time.

5. Do not count:
   - words the child self-corrects.
   - words pronounced differently in a child's dialect.
   - words the child repeats while reading (repetitions).

6. Calculate the Percent of Accuracy for a record by subtracting the total number of errors made from the number of running words in that text. That answer will be divided by the number of running words in the text.

   Running Words − Total Errors = Score

   Score ÷ Running Words = Percent of Accuracy

7. Compare the Percent of Accuracy to the chart for Defining Instruction on each record of reading behaviors to determine whether the child is reading at the predicted instructional level. You may wish to recheck the child's performance with another book at that level, or move the child to a higher or lower reading level based on this comparison.

8. Analyze the individual errors to make a prescription for specific skills and strategies you will explore with the child.

9. Use what you find out in Steps 7 & 8 to review the current guided reading groups in which children participate, to ensure that the groups bring together children with similar reading skills and strengths.

10. Place the finished records in children's assessment portfolios to use when conferencing on a child's progress.

Fruit Salad
22 Running Words

✓ ✓ ✓
I like apples.

✓ ✓ A |
I like oranges.

✓ ✓ ✓
I like bananas.

✓ ✓ apples T |
I like pears.

✓ ✓ pears SC
I like peaches.

✓ ✓ ✓
I like grapes.

✓ ✓ ✓ _____ |
I like fruit salad.

22 − 3 = 19
19 ÷ 22 = .86
or 86% accuracy

Record of Reading Behaviors

◯ = page number

Number of Running Words: 31

Playing (Level 1)

Book Title (Level)

Date:

Name:

② I like to run.

③ I like to hide.

④ I like to jump.

⑤ I like to slide.

⑥ I like to swing.

⑦ I like to crawl.

⑧ I like my bath best of all!

Noting Errors		
correct		✔ ✔ my eyes?
miscue		the ✔ my eyes?
insertion		✔ big ✔ my ^eyes?
omission		__ ✔ my eyes?
repetition		✔ R ✔ my eyes?
attempt		✔ e ey my eyes?
asks for help	A	✔ my eyes?
told word	T	✔ my eyes?
no response		_ ✔ my eyes?
self-corrects		the I SC ✔ my eyes?

See p. 100 for additional information.

Defining Instruction
95–100% Move child to higher level.
90–94% At comfortable instructional level.
0–89% Move child to lower level.

Calculating Percent of Accuracy

1. Running Words − Total Errors = Score

☐ − ☐ = ☐

2. Score ÷ Running Words = % Accuracy

☐ ÷ ☐ = ☐ %

Recommendation for Instruction: _____

Record of Reading Behaviors

Number of Running Words: 35

Book Title (Level) I'm Brave (Level 2)

Date:

Name:

② I'm brave.

I can catch

a lion.

④ I'm brave.

I can catch

a tiger.

⑥ I'm brave.

I can catch

a dragon.

⑧ I'm brave.

I can catch

a monster.

⑩ I'm brave.

I can catch

a bus.

Noting Errors

correct	✔ ✔
	my eyes?
miscue	the ✔
	my eyes?
insertion	✔ big ✔
	my ^eyes?
omission	__ ✔
	my eyes?
repetition	✔ R ✔
	my eyes?
attempt	✔ e ey
	my eyes?
asks for help	A ✔
	my eyes?
told word	T ✔
	my eyes?
no response	_ ✔
	my eyes?
self-corrects	the I SC ✔
	my eyes?

See p. 100 for
additional information.

Defining Instruction

95–100% Move child to higher level.
90–94% At comfortable instructional level.
0–89% Move child to lower level.

Calculating Percent of Accuracy

1. Running Words − Total Errors = Score

$$\boxed{} - \boxed{} = \boxed{}$$

2. Score ÷ Running Words = % Accuracy

$$\boxed{} \div \boxed{} = \boxed{}\%$$

Recommendation for Instruction: _____

Record of Reading Behaviors

Number of Running Words: 60

The Party (Level 3)

Book Title (Level)

Date:

Name:

② I'm having a party

with lots of balloons

and lots of hats.

④ I'm having a party

with lots of cakes

and lots of candles.

⑥ I'm having a party

with lots of cookies

and lots of ice cream.

⑧ I'm having a party

with lots of games

and lots of fun.

⑩ I'm having a party

with lots of friends

and lots of . . .

⑫ presents!

Noting Errors	
correct	✔ ✔ my eyes?
miscue	the ✔ my eyes?
insertion	✔ big ✔ my ^eyes?
omission	__ ✔ my eyes?
repetition	✔ R ✔ my eyes?
attempt	✔ e ey my eyes?
asks for help	A ✔ my eyes?
told word	T ✔ my eyes?
no response	__ ✔ my eyes?
self-corrects	the I SC ✔ my eyes?

See p. 100 for
additional information.

Defining Instruction
95–100% Move child to higher level.
90–94% At comfortable instructional level.
0–89% Move child to lower level.

Calculating Percent of Accuracy

1. Running Words − Total Errors = Score

☐ − ☐ = ☐

2. Score ÷ Running Words = % Accuracy

☐ ÷ ☐ = ☐ %

Recommendation for Instruction: _____

Record of Reading Behaviors

◯ = page number

Number of Running Words: ___

Book Title (Level) __Birthday Cakes (Level 4)__

Date: ___

Name: ___

② Tina had two candles

on her birthday cake.

③ She blew them out

with one big blow.

④ Lee had five candles

on her birthday cake.

⑤ She blew them out

with one big blow.

⑥ Chen had ten candles

on his birthday cake.

⑦ He blew them out

with one big blow.

⑧ Dad had forty candles

on his birthday cake.

⑨ He blew them out

with one big blow.

⑩ Grandma had lots of candles

on her birthday cake.

⑫ She blew and blew and blew.

⑭ "Quick," she said.

"Help me blow them out."

⑮ We blew them out

with one big blow!

Noting Errors

correct	✔ ✔ my eyes?
miscue	the ✔ my eyes?
insertion	✔ big ✔ my ^eyes?
omission	__ ✔ my eyes?
repetition	✔ R ✔ my eyes?
attempt	✔ e ey my eyes?
asks for help	A ✔ my eyes?
told word	T ✔ my eyes?
no response	_ ✔ my eyes?
self-corrects	the I SC ✔ my eyes?

See p. 100 for additional information.

Defining Instruction

95–100%
Move child to higher level.

90–94%
At comfortable instructional level.

0–89%
Move child to lower level.

Calculating Percent of Accuracy

1. Running Words − Total Errors = Score

☐ − ☐ = ☐

2. Score ÷ Running Words = % Accuracy

☐ ÷ ☐ = ☐ %

Recommendation for Instruction: _____

Record of Reading Behaviors

Number of Running Words: 131

Book Title (Level) Making Lunch (Level 5)

Date: _____

Name: _____

② "I'm making soup,"

said Uncle Vin.

"Who will help me?"

"Not me," said Sam.

"I'm too busy."

④ "I'm making sandwiches,"

said Uncle Vin.

"Who will help me?"

"Not me," said Anna.

"I'm too busy."

⑥ "I'm making orange juice,"

said Uncle Vin.

"Who will help me?"

"Not me," said Sam.

"I'm too busy."

⑧ "I'm making fruit salad,"

said Uncle Vin.

"Who will help me?"

"Not me," said Anna.

"I'm too busy."

⑪ "Can we have lunch now?"

asked Anna and Sam.

⑫ "No," said Uncle Vin.

"You were too busy

to help me make soup.

You were too busy

to help me make sandwiches.

You were too busy

to help me make orange juice.

You were too busy

to help me make fruit salad."

⑭ "You are too busy

to eat lunch,"

said Uncle Vin.

Noting Errors

correct	✔ ✔ my eyes?
miscue	the ✔ my eyes?
insertion	✔ big ✔ my ^eyes?
omission	__ ✔ my eyes?
repetition	✔ R ✔ my eyes?
attempt	✔ e ey my eyes?
asks for help	A ✔ my eyes?
told word	T ✔ my eyes?
no response	__ ✔ my eyes?
self-corrects	the I SC ✔ my eyes?

See p. 100 for additional information.

Defining Instruction

95–100% Move child to higher level.
90–94% At comfortable instructional level.
0–89% Move child to lower level.

Calculating Percent of Accuracy

1. Running Words − Total Errors = Score

[ ] − [ ] = [ ]

2. Score ÷ Running Words = % Accuracy

[ ] ÷ [ ] = [ ] %

Recommendation for Instruction: _____

Record of Reading Behaviors

Number of Running Words: _____

Book Title (Level): _____

Date: _____

Name: _____

See p. 100 for additional information.

Noting Errors

correct	✔ ✔ my eyes?
miscue	the ✔ my eyes?
insertion	✔ big ✔ my ^eyes?
omission	__ ✔ my eyes?
repetition	✔ R ✔ my eyes?
attempt	✔ e ey my eyes?
asks for help	A ✔ my eyes?
told word	T ✔ my eyes?
no response	_ ✔ my eyes?
self-corrects	the I SC ✔ my eyes?

Defining Instruction

95–100%   Move child to higher level.
90–94%   At comfortable instructional level.
0–89%   Move child to lower level.

Calculating Percent of Accuracy

1. Running Words − Total Errors = Score

☐ − ☐ = ☐

2. Score ÷ Running Words = % Accuracy

☐ ÷ ☐ = ☐ %

Recommendation for Instruction: _____

Dear Family Member:

I'm happy to share the news that your child is ready to start learning to read!

As part of our program for beginning readers, we will be using the *AlphaKids Guided Readers*. These child-friendly books offer brand-new readers step-by-step support, a world of charming stories, and real-life information. Every day, we'll be working together in small groups on phonics, reading comprehension, and word meaning as we read. That way every child will get the individual attention he or she needs for a quick and successful start as a reader. We'll also be sharing books with you, so that you can be part of your child's success. So be prepared. Very soon, your child will come home proudly proclaiming, "I can read!!!"

Sincerely,

_____

P.S. Parents often ask me how they can help their child get a good start in reading. Here are some of the ideas for fun reading activities I share:

• Find a few minutes to read, in a fun and friendly way, with your child in books of his or her choice. Let your child see you reading, too.

• Point out signs and read them out loud as you drive or shop together. Encourage your child to read the signs with you.

• Share nursery rhymes, poems, and silly songs with your child. Rhymes help your child hear the sounds of language in an enjoyable way.

Have fun with this and your child will have fun, too!